Written in the Cards
A very personal card reading

Madeline Escu

ISBN: 978-1-7391440-5-0

Olcan Press

First published by Olcan Press on 15th May 2023

Olcan Print/Press are a subsidiary of the Olcan Group

6 Park Hill, Ealing
London, W5 2JN, UK
Email: team@olcan.co
www.olcan.co

For permission contact:
team@olcan.co

A CIP record of this publication is available from the British Library.

First printed May 2023
Paperback ISBN: 978-1-7391440-5-0

Table of Contents

UNFOLDING MEMORIES

Taking a walk on Memory Lane

I love books! I grew up with books. I cried and laughed with books. I love to connect with the person behind the book, to wonder who she / he is, how she / he is behind the loneliness of the words. I think we are all living books - some unwritten, others forgotten.

The invisible narrator of your personal story is the best companion when you take the train in the morning to go to work and you are barely awake. The storyteller that lives inside your mind who oversees the happy endings…and the sad ones.

Sometimes it gets claustrophobic to live inside ourselves, in our own life story. The story we choose to tell ourselves about us gets used like an old vinyl and new sounds appear accidentally in the cracks of overplayed songs.

Random memory gaps filled with clay. In the morning, when dreams are still there and reality rises in dusk, we start creating our destiny like a hardworking spider, over and over again. We create fiction, into the cracks of our reality. When we really feel trapped into our own web of fiction, we go and see somebody who can clear us out: a psychologist, a therapist or a tarot reader. I chose the tarot reader for the simple fact that the cards have pictures and it's a fun process!

Let's meet!

That moment when we meet somebody and they tell us their name, most of the time we immediately forget it. This is because, at a first glance, we focus on the face of the person, the gestures, the sound of the voice, the body posture, the way they look at us. The name doesn't matter, but the feeling that person awakens in your body, the first impression, that magic moment when you know if he or she will stay forever in your life or if he or she will be a silent passenger crossing your road.

My invisible friend, let's create MAGIC together! My name has no importance.

How can we create magic? Which trick to choose? A deck of cards? A hat and a rabbit? A black cat?

Let's just pick a card and wonder if it's fate or just an accident. Are you a believer? Have you ever met a tarot reader? Have you ever eaten a fortune cookie? If you are a believer, you should also know that the whole principle is based on the law of attraction. We walk through life like magnets. Imagine a tiny magnet full with staples, pins, coloured buttons and stardust.

You are here, reading this book thanks to the law of attraction. Just be here and let the cards speak!

2. THE QUEEN OF CUPS: HAMSA!

The signs of cups in tarot are linked to emotions, intuition, and creativity. When the Queen (Mother) of Cups appears in a Tarot reading, you are being asked to listen to your heart. Stay open to your dreams because there is a world out there unfolding through your intuition!

Last year, during the pandemic, I took a yoga teacher training. When I finished the course, my teacher gave me a mantra: *"hamsa"*. *"Hamsa"* means "White Swan", which is the symbol of spiritual grace and majestic purity. The mantra's significance comes from the fact that, when we breathe slowly, the inspiration and the expiration are similar to the wings of a swan flopping in the morning mist, floating in the wind, imperceptible, melting into the mirroring water, leaving no trace in the air. The *"Hamsa"* mantra helps us find the grace within. Or another word for grace that could mean bliss, spirit, God or any kind of higher form of inspiration.

After a month of COVID-19 lockdown has passed, I found myself in a place near Paris and near the banks of the Seine. My only happy moments during this period were composed of sunlight, multi-coloured leaves, the wavy, ever-changing currents of the Seine, and the water birds. I used to ride my bike along the Seine, and just stop and watch the birds, fishing, flying, floating, and soaking in the sun. It is such an amazing gift to be able to float on water and ride air currents with the same ease. Water birds are fascinating. In a way or another, all birds are fierce predators - even the tiny ones, we should not be deceived by their fragile appearance.

Birds are also social, loud and vibrating characters (but not the swans - they are silent, as the secret of their perfect grace is actually this white silence). Sometimes, I was watching the ducks, the male and the female, always floating together, hanging around with the lazy swans, sitting on one leg by the shore, cleaning their feathers with their beaks, swirling around with their long necks, shining under the late November sun.

During this lockdown, the ducks from the parks took over the concrete city jungle: walking around on the streets like an army made of proud soldiers, conquering unknown human territory. I wonder if we were to hide from this coronavirus for much longer, would nature prevail and replace our footsteps with wild crawlers' invasion, a post-Chernobyl Apocalypse.

2020, COVID-19's year, was not as devastating as the year

of the plague, or the Spanish flue or chickenpox. It was more…. disturbing than devastating. Just like the loud ducks, we are social animals. Or maybe just social. I think that was our price to pay to avoid a global catastrophe: our solitude. The year of unrequired solitude. Just a random gift, offered by overwhelmed politicians and unanswered medical security questions. As most of all important life's choices, it was a random pick: to isolate the people.

Since childhood, I learned that being alone in nature is a way of cheating on the concept itself. My cure for loneliness is out there in the wild. Recently, during every sunny day, I took the bike and went out on the banks of the Seine, meeting the Water birds, enjoying the spectacular show of aquatic everyday life. I was wondering why the swans curl their wings in a heart shape, like the sails of a boat, while sliding through water with so much ease. Then, I noticed the young Grey swans, with their long geometric necks, carved like wood, as an indigenous sculpture: a big bird with no symmetric form and no obvious grace.

As any small, exquisite form of bliss, it sometimes comes out from the appearance of an ugly duckling; Like any beautiful sculpture that came out of a raw, uncut, compact piece of stone. I do not think that we are born beautiful. I believe we become beautiful. When I refer to beauty, I do not mean the esthetical way, but the existential way, as Sartre called it *"the becoming of the self";* the act of creation that we manifest every time we become master of our own destiny, when we wonder and question all establishment.

The lesson of the Swan is that you unfold your inner beauty with time and experience; you become one's true nature. In spring, summer, autumn, winter and…spring. Again and again.

What the year of the pandemic took from us was our capacity to move freely in space, and reduced us to playing in a small territory, like housecats. The difference between us and the housecats is measured by the level of resilience. Cats are way better at it.

"Hamsa": "Ham" - I flip the wings of my imagination, *"Sa"* - I exhale the story that was floating suspended in small particles of time. In this confined space, time expanded and left to another kind of place: the one of memoires and tales. My stories of the seasons that passed. The Queen of Cups (the swan) invites us to dive into de delicious chalice of inspiration.

In an incredible old fashioned way, Homer started the Iliad with the invocation of the muse who inspired him. Most of ancient Greek poets had these rituals of connecting to the sacred muse. Creation is never a lonely act.

"Speak, Memory —

Of the cunning hero

The wanderer, blown off course time and again

After he plundered Troy's sacred heights.

Speak

Of all the cities he saw, the minds he grasped,

The suffering deep in his heart at sea

As he struggled to survive and bring his men home

But could not save them, hard as he tried —

The fools — destroyed by their own recklessness

When they ate the oxen of Hyperion the Sun,

And that god snuffed out their day of return

Of these things,

Speak, Immortal One,

And tell the tale once more in our time."

On the day I asked my Memory to speak, my muse was away; maybe she was playing around in somebody else's story. As most of the important things in life, it was a random accident in an ordinary day that had me start writing. Therefore, I will tell you only the stories I pretend to know: mine! Let' pick another card! Choose wise!

3. FIVE OF CUPS: NOSTALGIA LANE

Dwelling into the chalice of feelings, the Five of Cups is the card of resentment, of sorrow and unapologetic nostalgia. It is a mourning card. But there can also be sweet poetry in melancholy.

When I came into my companion's life, he did not realize that he brought into the house a savage, a stranger. We lived this way: I was untamed, regardless of all the effort I made to adapt. I was coming from "a tribe" and he was a loner. I came from Venus and he was from Mars. We had it all wrong, but we possessed a lot of goodwill to make this work.

Our relationship is based on guilt. His guilt that he could never desire me and my guilt for never having the guts to leave him. We are so mainstream when it comes to mutual respect, a fake balance of gestures and words. It is like going to a Sunday church and sharing platitudes with everybody. Like an acrobatic performance where you walk an invisible wire on the top of a void. We are so kind to each other and attentive, in order to avoid the clash when I can have a Tourette crisis, one of the moments when I vomit my frustration and sadness. Ten years of my life of being polite, while I am just an uneducated white trash.

Fear. It is incredible how it can place us in the middle of the stage and point the finger on us. I can just hear hysterical laughter on my back and the audience going mad… Silent all these years, with no apparent reason except for guilt. Not strong enough to run away… or maybe just lazy.

I get my hugs in the morning and in the night-time, like a consolation prize: "Look, we are not having sex, but we have these cuddling moments to compensate!" Lately, the hugs make me sad - they feel like a morning ritual for my sexuality and youth. As good as it gets, isn't it nice? Cuddling in this dark, gloomy silence: these are the hugs of a killer for his prey, before he took the life out if it, before pulling the trigger. He avoids my body, like I was sick and suffered from a deadly disease. Like my body reminds him about his man failure, a fallen masculinity myth.

At the end of the day it's not about sex, it's about honesty. When I met him, I was so in love of my idea of "him". The big flood of imaginary romance rushing through my head. I was high on love infatuation. I used to spend my teenage years dreaming about lovers finding themselves, celestial bodies, coincidence's magic, and fusion spirits. How could I refuse myself the chance to live the biggest humanity dream: L.O.V.E? Poets sang about the glory of it, my favourite authors praised it and my soul was lingering for The One. Especially because I was turning 30, it was time to settle down, as written in the special column for single ladies in Cosmopolitan. By now, I can testify that L.O.V.E. is the most feared enemy of L.O.V.E. I'm no longer a romantic; I just want it real and raw.

I remember that one day he told me he is afraid that I am going to see him how he really is. That day came, but it was too late for honesty. Politeness came in and my golden cage started to build itself out of unspoken words.

The bigger the silence, the brighter the cage! A cage made from living illusion; a magic pot where I put to boil a raven's feather, the eye of the black cat, words, stories and the most important the strongly breaded net of my projections on love and relationships and others' expectations.

Lately, I started staring out the window. What if my story is not over yet? What if one day, I will glow into my blasphemy river and puke my shamed body on the floor, like sparkling diamonds? What if the thing that is really hurting me does not understand the situation, losing the point, my own blissful ignorance? What if the wound is the place where the light comes in? Waiting for the boiling point!

4. THE MAGICIAN: EVERY WITCH HAS A BLACK CAT

The Magician is the first card of the tarot deck. It is the beginning of your story. He is the father of infinite possibilities in a world where humans and animals talk.

The magician card is represented in this deck by a feline - because cats in ancient Egypt and Greece were believed to have magical powers to the extent that they could even bring the deceased back to life. Therefore, the say they have nine lives and an infinite possibility of action.

One day, an amazingly beautiful man came into our restaurant. He looked like an urban Viking, accompanied by his Irish setter on the name of Moos Milo. I was making conversation just to extend his presence infinitely. He asked me if I would love to adopt the baby cat that he found at the countryside a week ago, Meow Meow. At that point, I was ready to have his babies, so the cat was no problem! A week after, he came in with a black kitten. He said "don't worry, he has a white spot on his neck, it's called the Hand of God! He is no evil!" I made him a pizza and that was the price I paid for my cat. From that moment, he was the Pizza Cat.

I have never been a cat person. Cats back home in Romania were loud, savage and untamed; they used to steal food and developed no attachment. Dogs are faithful, kind, and they walk around with you. In the kingdom of animals, cats have a double nature - predator and prey. I read an article that explained the fact that if you die in a room with your cat, there is a strong probability you will be eaten by it!

I called my cat Gusto Cat, as he was a restaurant cat and that was the name of the venue. We tried to hide him from the customers - an animal in a restaurant is never good news, so we kept him in the office downstairs. In the night-time, I was so anxious until the last customers left, so I can free Gusto and play. I used to have highchairs in the restaurant, and he loved jumping on them and attacking me. I started to lengthen my stay at the restaurant with one more hour every night; just to play a little bit more with Gusto. I was not feeling like going home; there was nothing there to entertain me! But this crazy kitten needed a buddy. So did I. So we started hanging out together.

With time, we let him in the restaurant and people loved him! And he loved attention! He became a royal kitty, proudly greeting guests in his house. He became lazy, as an advantage of his majesty. His previous owner made me promise that I will never let him become a fat housecat. Well, I failed that promise…This black little Buddha is a restaurant cat, therefore he loves to eat. He is an Epicurean cat without a doubt! Still, half bulimic - because raised between humans, he copied their habits; he is a cat with eating disorders.

I ended up having a restaurant by accident, like so many other things in my life, but when I had Gusto, going to work was just a pretext to pet my fluffy royal hairball. In this kingdom of humans, Gusto taught me that we animals share so many things in common, and this royal kitty will die without affection as easily as he will die without food.

Apparently, my alter ego has the form of Cat! A friend of mine asked me once if I purr, because my alter ego kitty gets out and play sometimes. I imagined that my inner kitty self will do that naturally.

When you seed an idea in my head, it probably gets a few branches is no time. I was walking on Louvre Rivoli and thinking about it. About power and submission, the animal kingdom hierarchy, predators and prey; and on humans and relationships, the way we place each other in the garden of life. The more I walked, the more I felt taller. The kitty purr transformed into a roar.

I am a big cat: cute in a way, but ferocious and merciless as a hunter. I am a survivor, a prey animal with pretty sharp teeth. It is not a question of power or an ego statement. It is more accepting that you roar instead of purring and letting that voice out into the wilderness of the city life. In a way, we are all cats - predators and prey.

I Bet Gusto also feel he is not a fluffy overweight kitty, but a blue-black ferocious puma. Will Gusto eat me if I die?

5. THE HIGH PRIESTESS: THE FLOWER THAT TURNED INTO A SAINT

The High Priestess holds into her hands the secrets of life and death. She has the key to all secrets of life, and her mother language is compassion.

My grandma's name was Flower - an amazing name. She had dark skin, so we always suspected her to be a gypsy girl with blue eyes. Her skin was also amazingly soft and warm and even now I can feel her small hands holding me. It was not just a touch, it was a feeling.

When she held me in her soft arms, her hands turned into pure, melted love.

When I was a child, I used to spend most of my time in grandma's house. She had a drawer full of old buttons and tiny objects that served no purpose and I used to spend a lot of time searching for hidden treasures in it. The room had a window with a view of an amazing walnut tree, which represented to me the Tree of Life, because I was waiting for the morning light that came in with all my heart. I was so thrilled by that sight: the beginning of a new day, of a whole world of adventures that was opening to me. The oldest memory of Grandma is when she used to cradle me on her legs, on a small pillow, swinging me from side to side. From that moment on, I developed a strong passion for swings.

Flower worked in a bakery shop and, in the morning, when she was coming home, she smelled like bread. When she was young, she lost her first son to the God of Death and, at the same time, a part of her heart. From that moment, Sadness became her faithful companion and very often I could see tears in her eyes. Grandma was a religious person, because God also lost his Son and he understood her. The church was on the hill above the house and we could hear the bell tolls every Sunday. She used to tell us stories about Jesus and the saints and created this vision in my mind of all this biblical village and a stairway from the sky, on which Mary the Virgin and the saints were going up and down. Sometimes, in my dreams, I was walking around on these stairs, talking to all these characters. She taught me to pray to my guardian angel every night and I was sure he was around. He walked by my side until college, when he got super dirty after a party, lost few wings, and disappeared very ashamed of himself because he failed at his job to protect me.

When Flower lost grandpa, she refused to go back to her

old house. She told everyone that a snake made his nest inside it. It was the Snake of Loneliness. She moved in with her younger daughter and slowly she got tired of this situation and decided she will be the child, not the mother. Adulthood can be very oppressing sometimes. So, one day she felt like she could not walk anymore. Because she was not walking towards something, she decided to stop. The Snake of Sadness snitched through and pain came along. We had her registered in a care home. She died alone. Or maybe with Virgin Mary and the saints who came down on the stairway that day. When you endure so much pain in your life, you eventually become a Saint.

The day we lost grandma was actually the day when we truly found her, because we faced her pain: the pain of losing a loved one.

6. SIX OF SWORDS: CHARON AND THE MAGIC DESTINATION

Six of Swords represents progress - moving into calmer waters, moving on/ or moving forward. It can mean that you are experiencing a transition, but one that it feels natural. You are following the course of your life path. And Charon is taking you to the other side of the river.

The one who waits for me at the train station. At the airport. Who picks me whenever I come back to my home country? Mache, my Charon.

I remember when he appeared into our lives - I was not ready… I was just a child and Margot was my aunt. She was my "second mother" and she raised me like a daughter, her Bird of Paradise. There were so many stories and so much love involved! When he came into our lives, I did not quite understand the reason. Margot liked him, she was happy. He moved in.

Grandpa had a cherry tree in the middle of the garden where we used to play. The tree was very old, and, at some point, they had to cut it, so they can build a house for the newlyweds on that ground. Mache came into my childhood territory, and, in a selfish way, I was not happy about it, because it became his playground.

Time passed, and I started going to high school. Mache drove me there - he took me out from my childhood territory into the world. He continues to drop me off and pick me up from all my life adventures. He was always there to take me home and when I saw that his hair became white, I felt the time passing on all of us. He is my Charon, but the boat goes to Paradise, which I call home, the cherry garden blossoming of sweet memories.

7. THE EMPEROR: GO OUT IN THE WOODS

The Emperor card means authority, organization, a father figure. He rules in a man's world, he enjoys power and order. He is the patriarch. The father who gives structure to his kingdom!

Grandpa was raised in our town since his childhood. He saw the Second World War passing through, as some Germans stayed at his house. One of them had a horse and grandpa inherited it after the war. Not later, the collectives came and gathered all the horses left from the enemy.

He came from a family of hunters and he knew the forest around the house like no one else, and also its stories. During communism, hunting was forbidden. It was considered some sort of alternative economy, where people live from forest supplies instead of waiting at queues for bread portions. His father in law was also a hunter and, one day, police came to ask him where he hides his venison supply. It was hidden in the oak barrels that they used for wine making or sauerkraut. They beat him until they broke his ribs.

The forest was our neighbour, so more than one day a week we woke up in the morning, put on our rubber boots and took off for a walk. During summertime, after a rainy day we were picking up all sorts of mushrooms. Grandpa knew them all: the good and the bad, the amanitas and the boletus. He knew all the trees in the forest, all the secret pathways. Every place had a story - hunting or a war story, even if both have their resemblance.

Working as a truck driver when he was younger, he killed someone by accident, so he spent some time in jail. He came back with a lot of funny songs which he used to sing me while hiking in the forests. The only memory he wanted to share from prison or maybe the only one that he wanted to keep to himself.

While time passed, his heart went weak. He walked slowly, the hills became enemies, and he stopped a lot in order to catch his breath. At some point, his heart half-stopped. Only one side of him got tired, so he remained halfway paralyzed. He died not a long time after and everybody said that it was due to the black magic of my grandma because she didn't want to take care of him.

Grandma was a considered to be a witch and all the neighbours were afraid of her black spells. People said she could freeze water and all sorts of weird stuff. Grandma made a pact with the devil and she paid for it later on when we found her hanged in the garage. Police said they found animal blood on the scene, and dark marks on the wall. I'm still an atheist at this point, not looking for a religious explanation. I just think that grandma was lonely and sad and she believed in the invisible.

Once I had a dream. I was waking up with grandpa next to me, on a forest hill. At some point, he stops and says: "I cannot do it anymore. From now on, you father is going to be your guide in the forest". And so it was. Dad came in and took me further into the heart of forest. He was teaching me to read the trails, to be silent, to walk softly, to stalk and ambush, and to understand the sounds in the dark. If grandpa was taking me into the daylight, dad was walking with me in the dusk and into the night. When you leave home by dawn.

Out of the garden, you could walk straight into the forest and the whole animal kingdom rose in the tall grass of summer .There is something so special about sunset and nature, a kind of sooth vibration when humans and animals meet on the same territory. The light invites you in different dimensions; you walk slowly not to make any noise, not to disturb the deer jumping in the tall grass, wiggling their ears in the air.

Some days we could walk for two hours just to arrive at a precise spot where Dad decided we were on an animal path and we were going to wait there. He fell asleep most of the times and I used to look around and be afraid and amazed, sure that the fairies of the forest are not far. But I was also spooked by every little sound of a creeper on dry leaves. When night falls and you wait in the middle of the trees for your prey to come, even a mouse feels like a raging elephant. When you are a child in the dark and your parent just fell asleep because his day was hard, all sounds become symptoms of fear. The only nights where I felt safe were the nights when the moon was leading the way between the branches of the trees and the hills were gently caressed by her velvety light. In that darkness, there was not only nature, but something more, unexplained, but present. I yearned to be a crepuscular creature, wandering around from dusk to dawn, when the perfect moment for magic to manifest.

One afternoon, my father and I were waiting for deer to pass. We were sitting behind a tree, and I felt like talking, but he told me to shut up. Two deer came down the hill. I watched one of them in the eyes. Dad pulled the trigger. She tumbled, still looking me in the eyes. Death felt so simple. Years after that, I become vegetarian! Meat was not that important anymore.

Sometimes, on Sundays, we went out hunting with his friends. I was a 13 years old baby girl surrounded by old hunters. I was a special child in their eyes, and they used to give me strong alcohol served in tiny bottle caps; size matters, but also the age. When I shot my first rabbit, I was baptized as a hunter. You hold the rabbit on your back, and they hit you with a rod. I understand now that taking a life should be punished, and you hold on your back the weight and the pain of a kill. Back then, I was happy because I was a part of this male brotherhood which I admired so, I wanted to do my best to make them proud. Their little hunter girl. I wanted to be part of their legends and I am sure Dad still tells the stories of our adventures.

For me, being a girl was something so hard to accept. When my teenage breasts started growing, I felt terrible. I hated my period, the make-up, dressing up, being cute just to please the boys. I was one of the boys! One day, I took a shortcut in the forest and a weird guy followed me. I could hear him walking behind me and, suddenly, I felt like prey. When the hunter becomes the hunted is less fun. I started to speed up the pace and I was almost home. But then, he grabbed my T-shirt. I pushed him and fought back. Out of nowhere, I found myself on the ground and hardly could get up and run away. I came back home with a ripped T-shirt, felt so dirty and took a shower. Men - my heroes can be pure violence. It took me a long time after that moment to be able to walk by myself in the forest, without feeling like somebody was following me. Maybe it was just my guardian angel… playing pranks on me.

When Dad heard about it, he got furious, as he knew the guy - a half retarded looser whom he went to search for and kicked his ass. Dad was my hero.

Later on, I met men's violence in many forms. When I took the night train to go to college, it used to be full of weird characters. We were six persons in a booth, all crowded together in a hot smelly place, and with our skin sticking on red plastic couches. When we were lucky, we were two or three inside and we could lay down and grab some sleep in very uncomfortable positions.

Sometimes, I hoped to have a woman in the booth, because being with only men around me felt weird. The train attendant was the creepiest of them all, real predators. I don't even want to imagine all the girls, crowded in small corners having to pay their price for a train ticket… One night I was taking the train to Cluj-Napoca and by the last hour of my trip I remained alone in the booth with a man and we started talking. I knew that talking always helps with keeping men out of violence, out of breaking your body in two just because they felt like it and they could. Talking didn't work this time, as he took it as flirting and just jumped on me and started kissing me. The only thing that came to my mind was to tell him that I was a virgin, even if I was not. Apparently, talking works a little, as he just put a hand in my jeans and started touching me against the window. I just looked on the window as we were arriving in Cluj-Napoca and at the old abandoned factories, rusty metal, broken glass; blue sky and then morning came.

Morning light saved me when as we arrived in the station. I felt scared and excited at the same time. Thinking about it, aroused me. And frightened me. Violence is so ambivalent.

8. DEATH: KILL BILLA

In tarot, Death is not a bad card. It's more about rebirth and renewal. While letting go of our attachments to the past, we are starting fresh a new chapter of our life. It is about spiritual transformation that leeds to freedom. Free as a wild horse!

"We rode horses made of sticks

He wore black and I wore white

He would always win the fight

Bang bang, he shot me down

Bang bang, I hit the ground

Bang bang, that awful sound

Bang bang, my baby shot me down"

(Nancy Sinatra, "Bang Bang")

Ever since I was a child, I have been a big fan of cowboys

and Indians books. My aunt Margo who is a literature teacher was always telling me: *"Stop reading that crap!"* But my heroes were riding horses in the Appalachia Mountains, talked to the trees, tracked footsteps on the ground and made fire out of dried leaves and fungus. I always dreamed of having a horse of my own.

When communism fell in 1989, it seemed like our regular lives got dismembered, post-Chernobyl kind of deserted spaces. The industry in our city just collapsed because the factories were working with the big Soviet bear. But we left the bear for the majestic eagle. All of a sudden, this dream of a better life outside the frontiers made all the young folks leave the country to go work somewhere in Europe, for better paid salaries and worse jobs. The city was scattered in leftovers of steel rusty factories, broken glasses, and hives of ivy and plants taking over. Nature always takes back her reign after the departure of humans.

The worst part of this post-communist apocalypse was that in the villages most of the people who remained were old people, not able to work abroad or even on the fields, in the forest. It was not bad enough the communism tried to bite the inner core of this majestic magic space that the Romanian village was. Capitalism finished the job.

I strongly see Romania like being stuck a century earlier than her other European cousins. In here, it is normal to see on the roads or between cars carriages with horses. In here, the agricultural revolution took its time and the mighty horse was winning over the steel machine.

But, in the beginning of the 90ies, so many things and beings got abandoned, the people found freedom outside the borders and ran away. And also the horses. They had no master anymore - they were free to run in the forest.

I was amusing myself with a group of friends and went in the forest with a few corn grains to try and catch a horse –

the most curious one. Then, with dexterity, I put a rope against his neck and rode it. We were riding wild horses with just a rope, lots of courage and a few falls and bruises.

There were days when I was walking in the forest trying to search for the wild bunch of abandoned and newly free horses. The most beautiful moment was the sunset when the orange light was sparking in their skin. I was just staying there on the hill, watching them being together, playing, fighting, caressing each other, just like family. I could have stayed there for an eternity, hearing their incomprehensible language of love, hate, motherhood, sisterhood and pride. Sometimes I was bringing then crumbs of bread and feeding them from my palm. It took a while to catch some courage, but they slowly came closer. This was my wild family. In my mind, that was the perfect impersonation of freedom and the joy that comes from within. Running wild, together.

When I turned 18, Dad bought me a baby horse. She was fiery red, like a soft sunset. I called her Billa Bobilla, because she loved eating the corn grains (in Romanian we call them "bobite") from the palm of my hand. In the beginning, I spent a lot of time with her in the stable in order to get to know her. I was brushing her back, avoiding the kicks and the bites, because she was just young and tempered.

I was studying for my Baccalaureate exam in the garden and she used to lay down near me in the grass. When she was going further in the fields, I whistled and she answered in her horse whining and came back to me. She had the bipolar personality of a horse and a dog. She had amazingly huge black eyes with long red eyelashes. I used to put my hand on her eyes and close them, feel the bump of her eyes rolling inside my palm. You need to really trust a human as an animal in order to close your eyes and let the fight or flight instinct aside and just rest your gaze into his palms. I was never forgetting to be careful because she had a temper and her trust came in a limited amount.

During winter time, she stayed mostly in the stable, but I was taking her out for walks, and she loved rolling in the snow. A huge red horse rolling in the white untouched snow with so much ease and much more joy.

We started riding together after she was 1 year old. In the beginning, she launched like a rocket, but with time she was listening to my body, feeling when my balance was unsteady, waiting for me. She took me one spring in an orchard of blossomed plum trees; she delicately walked me into this sea of smell and flowers. Unusual sounds were scaring her and then I had to hold her strongly in-between my knees, to make sure I will not lose my majestic throne of bones, movement and magic.

I was letting her run free in the forest with the other horses and from now and when I was searching for them; I always had my grains of corn and breadcrumbs. I whistled, she answered, and my heart jumped happily. Sometimes, it took me the whole day of walking until finding them. She made friends and she introduced me to her new family. This state of freedom I have seen in the middle of the forest continued to amaze me because I felt deep inside that in the reign of humans we can only have a temporary glimpse of what this really feels like (if we are lucky).

I never sat a saddle on her, only my rope and my knees kept tight on her ribs. Sometimes, she was all sweaty and she smelled of wildlife and hay. I was my own little Appalachian Indian riding my red silver horse on Romanian hills. Indians believed that looking through into somebody's eyes you can have a glimpse of his soul. Freedom vas her soul. I just think she gave me that love of moving freely.

It is not impossible to ride a dream. Do dreams really come true? If you believe strong enough, they do, but not in the way you imagine. They manifest in a random shady way like a sparkle of light on water. There are here now, for a moment, and then they're gone in a perpetual movement of light kissing the darkness of water.

Today, I had an enormous headache and I felt like writing. I took a walk in the forest and Billa came back. She wanted to be reborn out of my head like Athena out of Zeus' head. She wanted to jump out of my head and gallop freely on dried leaves, on the moist autumn ground after I set her loose.

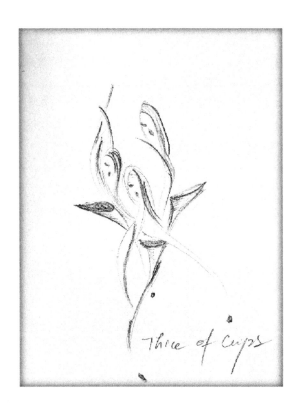

9. THREE OF CUPS: HAPPY TREE FRIENDS

Three of Cups is all about celebration, friendship, and alliances. It's about a circle of women who make magic sparkle. Your tribe of soulmates getting together. This card reminds us that your group identity is a part of who you are.

"I got caught in a storm

And carried away.

I got turned, turned around,

I got caught in a storm.

That's what happened to me.

So I didn't call,

And you didn't see me for a while."

(Lhasa de Sela, "Rising")

The singer Lhasa de Sela died in 2010 of breast cancer. She resembled a lot with my friend Cosmina, who also kneeled 5 years ago in the face of cancer. I was not there with her. This is a letter I got from her back in 2012:

"Do you know what I feel? That dream in which I die, but I continue living. I feel like I will live like that until the end of time, a life that doesn't belong to me, a life that I don't want and it doesn't regard me. I will have no kids in this lifetime. Just solitude for me. I am not complaining, it's just the reality inside my soul. I'll be sad and lonely as long as I will be able to bare this.
I feel lonely and strange, like a convict in his own life."

This is what I answered:

"Bubu, just stop with all this bullshit. You have to fight for what you believe in, don't give up! We all have passed through difficult years. Just hang in there! Inside of you, there is a fighter, this is just a life lesson. Just take it easy, be patient.
One day, you will have a family and kids, one day you will be loved again! Just stick there for the spirits to come back. Stop torturing yourself with blame, stop being your own punisher. Put your crazy judgemental ego on mute. Relax, take a bath. You're the fighter, the one that our martial art teacher thought us to be! Come on, breathe! You have the power in you. I love you Bubu, you'll be fine. I'll be having your babies, but just chill! ☺"

Babies were an important thing to her because she had an abortion, because her boyfriend didn't want the baby. She used to talk to her unborn baby and that haunted her a lot, as the void in her belly left place for death. She died of ovary cancer.

Imagine baby birds in a nest, happy tree friends. Me, Cosmina and Oana - we were them. The first time we went out in a bar, we saw the ashtray on the on the table moving, no explanation, and we all three knew it: it was magic. Magic happens in triangles and circles. That kind of magic that comes when you fall in love and the whole world changes from grey to Technicolor. Not voodoo, but soft magic composed of sunset vibes, smiles, happiness and friendship.

Cosmina was beautiful, like an exotic flower walking in her own scent of youth and femininity. She was like a magnet to people, both men and women. I always found this fascinating, especially because by that time books were my friends and being feminine was that last of my interest. She was my Great Priestess in becoming a woman. We used to go school just to meet there so we can hang out. We had a coffee shop nearby and we were hanging around, sipping American coffees for three hours and smoking packs of cigarettes. We were students with no money.

We were against this post-communist capitalist Romania, ready to change the world. So, we imagined ideas of making a business together. We started organizing student parties every Thursdays in a bar. We gathered all people we knew, a heteroclite crowd, of punk, ravers, rappers, nuns, old, young etc. and we were laughing our asses off. We loved this life circus, made of colours, diversity, of bringing different people together and making social alchemy. We were dancing on that music like Valkyries, sharing imagined worlds and having a laugh. We once thought about opening a rabbit farm, because rabbits reproduce fast. The Absurd was hanging out with us like a character from Eugene Ionesco, he was our constant friend with whom we used to make fun of everything. Life is absurd, Romania is a big messed up country with no future and our laugh was a way of coping and hoping. The consensual world was boring and our gang's motto was *"it does not matter what matters, it only matters what doesn't matter"*.

We always imagined Cosmina as a business woman who later who would take her baby to the office in a backpack. At some point, she started hanging with the cool kids, the skaters and snowboarders, the stoners and the funky people. Everything was like a maze in which we lost her, a maze of weed and bullshit. She loved snowboarding and now, when I go in the mountains and slide on a perfect line of new snow, I feel her next to me.

We all know that baby birds are supposed to take their first flight into this world. We finished college and I took a job at an airline company, on booking flights. Oana lived with me and she waited for me every night with a bottle of red Cabernet. Every night, we drank a bottle of wine together and, at the end, Oana had revelations: *"when you pass out because of alcohol, you should always pass out on a side, in order to avoid choking with your own vomit"*. We were choking on no future life, no good jobs, on the promise land of mediocrity that we always feared.

Cosmina bought a car, on old pimp-car Mercedes. All three of us drove to the seaside. She was always stoned while driving that car and the ride felt weird. We arrived at the seaside, happy that we survived, at a nudist beach, where we smoke pot and jumped in the waves. Water felt like smooth velvety grass. We ran in rice fields, we floated, we laughed, and sunset was there. My best memory of her is her smile.

Mother Nature can be a harsh and cruel bitch, and sometimes not all of her babies survive. The eagles, the foxes and the night owls are out there hunting. One of us did make it, and payed the price for the dreams of a better world, payed the price of innocence.

Years after I realized - we don't own our destiny. Fuck meritocracy, it's a myth! We have a political destiny, the one with which you get born, the age, the country, the status and the gender. The whole social background that you cannot easily escape. Our destiny was that we were born in a country that strangled us. A country that nearly got out of a dictatorships and fell into a big messy need of unhuman values called Capitalism. Where you had the possibly to dream but not the reality to live the dream. A country which Oana and I left because she took the third of us down into the darkness. Sometimes running away is the only way.

10. THE EMPRESS: THE GENERAL WHO RULES BY THE FORCE OF KINDNESS

The Empress in a nurturer – for her family, friends, animals and even plants. She is the ultimate care-giver. She is the feminine principle incarnated. She is the Mother.

Women are nurturers. They are wombs and caregivers. They are unconditional love. When giving birth, a mother bear can be the most dangerous beast of the forest.

I am a lucky one, as I had two mothers. One was my aunt, a fresh-out-of-college young girl and the other one was her sister, my real mother, and fresh-out-of-birth-giving-pain.

My Mum had a few years ahead of miscarriages, of blood, violence and solitude. She couldn't carry a pregnancy until the end for a long time before she had me. Sometimes, the miscarriages arrived late. She was young and strong and my unborn brothers and sisters left no memories behind them. The only marks left are from my Dad's hands: big, hard, furious marks on her skin. Dark violet circles and lots of tears. Dad loved alcohol like a national sport, alcohol that blurred his mind and heated up the spirit.

My mother had a mother too. One day, Mum couldn't handle the beatings anymore, so she told Grandma that she was thinking of leaving her husband. She was beautiful, dark skinned, with almond eyes and long black hair. Grandma told her that she should go back to him, because they couldn't face the social pressure of what the world would say if about such separation. "The world" meaning the small city they lived in, the gossiping community in front of the bakery shop where my grandma worked. Shame is a big matter in our family, like in most of the families I think. It's like wearing a neat white dress on a bruised, beaten body, just to look nice. Mum returned to Dad and never left him since.

You don't contest your mother's advice because you think she is here in the world to protect you, to soothe you and to lead the way. They should know better, but sometimes they get it all wrong without intention.

After I was born, she was happy, but lost. The first baby is a challenge, especially when you have to go to work, clean the house, cook, take care of the garden, do the laundry and put up with a violent man. I always considered women who lived during communism heroes. The political model is that women and men work together, some sort of gender equality system. But then comes the twisted side: they were working together in the factory, but she was coming home and continued her housewife chores as a second shift - the night shift. As most of the mothers, she was underpaid. Life was hard, but she did complain, waiting for empathy, especially from other women. Women have ears that man don't have. The daily life became a matter of endurance, pain, resistance and resilience. At that time, suffering was a common noun. Suffering had dignity in it, something religious. "I have to carry my cross"- she sometimes said. My mother was a beautiful Pieta, as suffering for her children made sense and she had a purpose in life. Nowadays, we all seek happiness and fulfilment of our individual self. Happiness is a modern duty.

After a year and a half, my younger sister was born. She was an unexpected baby, because they were not ready for a second child. The abortion money was invested in a stereo player. This is how music saved my sister's life. By that time, abortion was illegal, and it was made in the patient's house, with rudimentary means by improvised midwives. All those unborn communist babies went straight back to Paradise through a bathroom window.

Two children can be a hard burden for a working class family. Besides their regular jobs, my parents had a small farm. We grew up with a garden full of sheep, pigs, cows, horses, chicken and geese. They grew tomatoes, plum trees, beans, salads and all sorts of veggies. They had double lives: one as workers in a factory and the other as farmers in the backyard of their house. Mother had a small village of domestic animals to take care of. She found the kindness those humans around her sometimes in those animals. Gentle, innocent and helpless creatures. All at the mercy of men. The big dark eyes of the calf with their pink muzzle were the cutest manifestation of life itself. Motherhood is a feeling that spreads around when a woman is designed to be a caregiver, a protector and a nurturer. The love my Mum had towards the animals on the farm was infinite. And they gave back, unlike humans. Their kindness was unconditional (or based on food ratio). There was no betrayal among them, no feelings of hurt, no cursing and swearing, no violence.

The hardest part of all was during wintertime when the ground became frozen, with dirty ice cracks under rubber boots. Hands hurt because of the cold, and at 7 o'clock in the morning it was still dark outside. Only living things are steaming white clouds of air in the mist of dawn. We were heating up the water for the animals to break the thick ice in their buckets.

Winter made everything so difficult. The only heated places in the house were the kitchen and the bedroom. Mum and Dad were sleeping in the bedroom and me and my sister on a convertible couch in the kitchen. When morning came and they had to go to work, we switched places and we took over the bed in the bedroom, half asleep like zombies. None of these things seemed unnatural, as the house was warm from the wooden fire that our parents sacredly kept alive during the night. Winter brought us together so close, and since childhood we learned that love is tactile, it comes through the skin, like as caress, like a hug in a nice cosy house during the hibernal season. Love is shelter.

The house smelled like cookies and all sorts of delicious treats Mum was cooking for all of us. Dad never cooked a meal in the house, nor he did laundry or cleaned. The domestic chores were for the wife. This way, Dad could be a baby just like us - cleaned, fed and nurtured. She also had access to all family's money and acted like our accountant. She paid the bills and did the shopping. In the matters of domestic life, Mum was a General who ruled by the force of kindness. Nowadays, we call this "soft skills. Maybe that's why Dad was brutal with her... probably because that was the only force he could use against her.

A caregiver and an alcoholic make a nice cocktail for a co-dependent relationship. Addiction comes in many forms. He was addicted to alcohol and she was addicted to the resentments and to the sorrow. When growing up, I became so obsessed and found myself into co-dependent relationships - apparently, that occur often when you have co-dependent parents. I kept my guard high and fortunately I didn't have many relationships, but some of them lasted long. The concept of co-dependent relationships also put me in the middle of it, and it is hard to admit that I lived it also... My parent's relationship was not a dysfunctional one, because by that time in rural Romania that was the norm. We were not living an exceptional, deviant destiny, but a rather a cool, moderated working class saga.

I was restless, the kind of child that challenges the unconditional maternal love. As first child in a family, I was smothered in affection and expectations. Dad wanted a boy instead of a girl, so he just educated me as a boy. My aunt wanted a brilliant child, so she had me reading by the age of 6. My mother wanted a girl to wear pink clothes and not get herself full of mud the first moment she stepped out of the house. I just wanted to please everybody, but I definitely hated pink dresses. I was a naughty feisty girl, loud and ópinionated, short tempered and stubborn. Pure joy for a parent. Mum and I used to fight a lot. She was all I didn't wanted to be and I made sure that she knew. That should hurt a lot... My first rebellion was against my Mum.

The passage from childhood through adolescence is an act of rebellion. Against that body which once was yours you stand up and ask for another. I was reading a lot and my heroines were the amazons, not the housewives. I was merciless and cruel. I still am - for me, a proof of love is to stir doubts and habits in the persons I love. I sometimes think that I know best, which is definitely wrong. Shouting is just another form of despair… After most of our fights, she used to cook me something nice and I took the peace offer. I was easy to bribe with food. Because when she ran out of words, she spoke in her love language by the means of cooking. Food never lets you down when needed.

I moved out to boarding school at the age of 14. Since then, I bounced back and forth from various places to home. Home became this miraculous oasis to which I returned every time I had a chance. Mum was planning her menu one day before my arrival. Home became nostalgia of a Paradise lost very early in my life. Travelling places, living with strangers, college dorms, solitude, and the big grey city made out of my childhood place my North Star. My green cocoon of warmth and magic knitted in memories and myths.

Like a big block of ice in the winter that needs some hot water to be melted, I kept my pain of leaving home solid. Between the ice crystals there are dried leaves, warm memories and a family who was not afraid to say I love you.

When you come back, it's hard to distinguish reality from fiction. I never let my mum change in my eyes… I closed my eyes for so many years, and in a way I lost her as a human and I kept her as my Mum. In a world ruled by a man (God), I contest this unique masculine energy of power, and I bow to the universal giving energy of The Mother, untainted, supportive energy that never lets you down and always holds your hand and nourishes your bones. My unique deity to which I bow is the Female, the protective womb of amniotic liquid in which my soul moves with ease.

11. THE QUEEN OF PENTACLES: THE LIFE BEFORE US

The Queen of Pentacles is the nurturing mother of the material world. It is a mother figure who can provide you with loving support and care.

What is your life journey? Can you imagine that one thing, that single life event that will profoundly define you? Who are you in your life's timeline? What is your greatest picture to hang at the entrance of your experience palace? Is it a Pieta, a Botticelli, a fat Renaissance baby angel or a Guernica of Picasso, a Hopper? What grand story made you who you are?

As I grew up next to my two mothers (my Mum and her sister), I can say that I was proudly raised in a family of amazons. Margot, my aunt, is a literature teacher. A big-time dreamer with a huge dose of sensitivity, with two children, a husband, one dog, hundreds of books and well-hidden packs of cigarettes.

She and I lived experienced together the fall of communism. I felt her joy, while not really understanding it as a child. She graduated college during oppressive Communist times with Magna Cum Laude, and she could choose to teach anywhere in the country, but she chose to come back to our small countryside hometown. When you have unfinished business with your childhood, you always come back to her territory, charmed by her spells and her traitorous beauty.

Margot gave me so many books to read and the biggest point in common we had been the belief that written words creates reality. Without any doubt we believed in magic.

If you were to reincarnate in a word what would it be? I would love to come back reincarnated in a point, because the point is limitless, an infinity of possibility. You can dive in a point, like a rabbit whole, like Alice in Wonderland or start knitting stories like a patient grandma around the fireplace before winter.

She loved this book written by Romain Gary, "The Life before Us", that told the story of a child named Momo and Madame Rosa, a former hooker. It is about her playing the mother role for the child and her slow and rough pathway to dissolution. When she dies, Momo writes: "she had stopped breathing, but it was all the same to me. I loved her even without breathing."

Margot made me read that book and told me "if one day I become a decrepit old woman, a vegetable, I will kill myself". That was serious business of her to say - tell me your fears and I tell you mine! My fear was to become a woman, a wife, a mother, and that is why I preferred to remain an eternal child, a Peter Pan. I sincerely believe that motherhood left deep scars in the hearts of the women in my family.

She became a wife and a mother, a really good mother for all of us and she faced the frustration of female gender roles, status-playing, and all the ridiculous political destiny of humans (white, Middle calls, Eastern European woman). A sort of disenchanted territory of frustration and shattered dreams. Still, she kept her secret garden of friends – her favourite authors, with good chats and frenzy, intelligent and emotional life. Margot just hid herself in the books and she went back to that lost territory of living- dreaming whenever she pleased.

When Grandpa died, my Grandmother moved in Margot's house, because in Romania one cannot simply send elder people to a care home, as it is unbelievably bad regarded by society, as a manifestation of pure selfishness and a subject to people's disgrace. Grandma moved in and she spent her lonely moments in Margot's kitchen, watching all her movements like a Sphinx, having an opinion about everything and every person that came visit her. But in a way don't all mothers do that to their children?

The whole concept of intimacy just got scattered away, she lost her private life, her secret hideaway, her nest. The observer, the judge, the inquirer was always there. There cannot be two ladies of the house, and grandma had the leverage of her age and experience on her side. A daughter and a mother, a saga of feminine characters acting as one single Mother.

With time, Grandma started to move less and less and slowly turned into an oversized mermaid. Her feet were useless for this world and the ocean was too far away… She started dwelling on the green algae-like coloured couch she was sleeping on. Her old friends were visiting her like in a weekly pilgrimage of chatting, exchanging news and sipping coffee. They were taking about who died lately, who got married, and making fun of others or themselves, happy grandmothers.

Meanwhile Margo became her private daughter-nurse. Sacrifice is a very important value in our feminine side of the family. We are born with the duty to take care of our elders – "I brought you to life" kind of duty, the one which nobody can escape. The debt of birth. A life debt!

Is it possible to hate someone as equally as the love is grand? Obviously, the answer is yes! The closer we are to somebody, the biggest the polarity attraction. Love is ambivalent. I love my mother as an open statement to my humanity, my childhood, and the memory of the skin. We are all at some point an extension of our mother's skin. Then, when that skin expands into your house, taking up your vital space to exist, to breathe and to manifest, darker feelings slide in: bitterness, resentment and despair.

Her green algae-like bed started to smell the shallow waters. She was like a stranded mermaid on the leftover of the tides. A book has no smell, or maybe smells like Proust's madeleine, vanilla or something pleasant and sugary. But you know it's real life hitting you when your nose turns out your stomach inside out. You want vomit everything: your feelings and your breakfast. Truth can only be realized in this dirty body. The body of sweat and tears, of joy and suffering. We are all dancing on the rope of our existence. Life in general lies between stardust and mud; same component, different smells.

How does it feel when all your ideals start decomposing into the fiercely light of time, a cruel reminder of your meaninglessness? When flesh abandons herself to the earth, slowly going back to where it came. Grandma was swimming into the shallow waters of an ocean being drained of waves, leaving behind small shells and the smell of the tides.

How can you morally accept that you want her gone already, that is disgustingly insane, because of mother love and all this ethical dilemma? Grandma Flower was bringing the tides into Margo's house and that was too much to bear for any human being. Life as it is can be more majestic or more grotesque than any book in the library. We all get to have this lesson that roots us deep into the ground, and it is not a lesson of loss, but more about acceptance. It is the beginning of adulthood.

While searching for the perfect mother love, going back repeatedly into this womb of pearly white kindness, we forget that mothers can also be reckless and selfish and uncoherent. We take them for granted just because they were before us.

One day, Grandma swam into the dark blue sea and never came back. She ran away with the other mermaids making fun and enjoying underwater gossip. Margot was devastated. The drama was gone, but also that place for tragedy was empty. The green algae couch was empty. All the ambivalent feelings appeared - the torture, the pity, the rage, and the love.

Sometimes, something outside of you can be so big that succeeds to invade your spirit, to haunt you and feed you with its blurry energy. Grandma took a lot of space, and that space had to be filled with something else. Knowing Margot, that place will be filled with books and motherhood. There is a mother role to play in the story, while learning from the mistakes of the past, the womanhood karma of the family.

Do not we all carry our resentful feelings, our failures, and our disillusion as Sisyphus carries his boulder at the top of the hill? But don't they make us a part of who we are? Instead of relating to an old ancient Greek story, what if Sisyphus could be happy? The rock is there as long as we hold on to it and then it's gone.

"You take a piece of stone, chisel it with blood, grind it with Homer's eye, and burnish it with beams until the cube comes out perfect. Next, you endlessly kiss the cube with your mouth, with others' mouths, and, most important, with infant's mouth. Then you take a hammer and suddenly knock a corner off. All, indeed absolutely all, will say what a perfect cube this would have been if not for the broken corner" (Nichita Stanescu)

This is the perfect cube. And so she is!

12. THE CHARIOT:
YOU WILL MEET A TALL DARK STRANGER

The Chariot asks you to consider the state of your ego. Have you become so set in your ways that you're missing the bigger picture? Are you rushing into life more than necessary?

My cousin and I are big fans of a tarot reader called Vera. She has long black hair and a beautiful voice that amazes us every time she is reading the cards for our zodiac signs. Because she is always bringing unpredictable and exciting news for us, the week after Vera's tarot reading is more fabulous than reality itself. It reminds me of that movie of Woody Allen, *"You will meet a tall dark stranger"*, in which the heroine makes a great caricature of herself and spices up her life because a fortune teller predicted an amazing love affair.

When I was living in Santorini Island in Greece, another fortune teller told me that He was the man of my life, and I believed her. 10 years after, I stand before "the man of my life", buffering like an old computer that cannot keep up the pace, drunk on the illusion of love and the life in between.

A few months ago, Vera also told me that I will meet the man of my life – definitely a fortune teller thing. Do they say it because their audience desperately dreams about it? Why is it always something about a man? My simplest answer would be that we all crave for a real man between our thighs. Nothing else matters, neither fortune, status, career nor morals. Beside all the cultural codes, nature has us all the way. A sneaky cunning bastard, made of hormones and adrenaline, a pleasure cocktail of sweat and scream.

Not a long time ago, I started chatting with a man on social media. We were friends on Facebook for a couple of years and we were talking random things. Let's call him Mr. X. He asked me all sorts of questions about myself. It was new; nobody asked that for a long time. We travelled in time, talked about our childhood, talked about dreams, wonders and desires. Suddenly, in my grey suburb life we created an imaginary coloured island for two strangers. There were birds, clouds and music. The sky rose over my head as a sea of emotions, fluffy feelings and lunar walks. Sometimes we were hanging around in clouds, watching the sunset, swinging on a string above the world. My dreamy mind was ecstatic, out of my dull faded relationship I could have run out every night in a fantasy land shared with a leprechaun.

Unfortunately, he was taking a lot of drugs which

explained his attraction to fantasy land, slippery colours and daydreaming. For me, all these things came naturally since childhood. We spent the two months of pandemic lockdown in this virtual territory. I became an Avatar of myself and we were virtually hanging around together until the morning birds and the crickets reminded us that we are real. When we were going to sleep in the morning, I imagined his hands around me.

When confinement was over, we found the time to meet and even more time to hug. I wonder what would have happened if I didn't fill the void and the loneliness of my couple with the sparkle of this new love. The sparkle of a firefly in the night searching for his mate, the sparkle of hope that not everything is lost or too late. That I still have a chance of passion in this life, that even if I fucked it all up, life will give me a chance to start all over. That I can dream again. I just hoped it could be that easy. Not to have to fight for it, go through a break-up, a new life's challenge, loneliness and lots of strangers. I hoped that I met my tall dark stranger.

The ironic part of it was that even when he really held me in his arms it all felt like a fantasy, a dream that became real, hugging me, breathing near me. How could I stand my loneliness for that long?

One day, he couldn't sleep because he was horny and apparently I am his fantasy while I am in the underground going to my yoga class. I entered the game with deep hot breath and the underground expands in this no time space. It was just me and him, touching our phone screen, screaming and moaning in our imaginary foreplay. There were no people left around me, just his presence lurking around. The memory of our bodies together sets the decor for this virtual intercourse. Desire is in the brain – this is our main sexual organ. Mind-fucking.

I never felt like an immoral adulterer or a cheater. It felt right. It felt sublime; no other fantasy land would beat the skin on skin feeling. *"We live in the best of all possible worlds"* Leibniz spoke through my head. The chemistry of two people in the beginning of their adventure is as strong as any drug, as addictive and destructive also. Desire's beginning is the sweetest poison that we can digest. I tasted that a few times in my life. But I wonder how you would avoid the power of desire that consumes its own flame until the bone, leaving behind resentment, broken dreams, and bitter loneliness. We end up loathing the thing that at some point we cherished the most. Falling in love is a matter of life and death. Facing the dark side of love – this is what comes along behind the mask of happiness. Thanatos out of the shady caves of hell, of sorrow and loss. The least but not last my strong conviction is that the best love stories are happening when you exit the scene before the end of the third act. Before the audience starts to get bored, waiting to get back home to their nice warm soup.

Why would you take the risk that the same object of love will make you suffer viscerally, will destroy you in time, like a silent but steady killer? I do not even think is the object, but the idea we make of love, living with one-other, monogamy, couples, gender roles and all the rest of the unwanted collaterals.

I thought for a moment that there is a lucky exit from my grey monogamous life, a stairway to heaven, with coloured florescent pebbles and firefly dust. Or maybe I did not believe in it… Did I turn my head as Orpheus just to make sure all this is real, to make sure that Eurydice is walking behind him? I'm full of doubt, I barely understood my choice of leaving it. I felt like he prefers Avatars, but I wanted to feel real, bone and skin, a dot in the present moment with infinite possibilities. I am here. Now. Presence.

I thought at the end of the stairway to romance the door was closed. Or was I Alice in Wonderland, too big or too small for the gate, with no key? Where is that key? My understanding of not making the same mistake again, or not understanding at all?

I realized that the moment I leave this soft cocoon of silence, I should know better in order not to make the same mistake again. Not to become unreal and invisible, a shadow. And silent. Silence is the killer of souls!

Or maybe my wounds, healed but not too strong yet, called me back in my cave of solitude. *"You're not ready yet!"*

Or he was not my Orpheus but more like a Charon taking me gloriously to the others side of my trapped life. Into Inferno, the place of all possibilities. All beginnings start with Death, a descent in Thanatos's world. The Devil - the card of the burning flesh, desire melting to the bone. I was losing myself into pure pleasure, abandoning into this union of fire. I was going back into my animal womb, connecting to the depths. of the flesh, to the beauty of being alive. Through the man who oppresses you there is always a response from the universe: a man that's setting you free.

It can happen that a person can be a Bridge between an old and a new relationship. He takes you over the tormented waters of solitude; he takes u up into the sky towards new horizons. I would think about tarot I would say that he was the Chariot. He took me into his Chariot with him, and while driving the horses of matter, of the flesh, and like a true alchemist he turned the matter into spirit, sky and ether. He offered me a ride to the other side. He was not romance, he was magic, scattered moments of a connection from the other side, he was a reminder of my connection with life, and he was me.

Deep in my heart, I know that when I will cross this torrent of life, nothing would stop me in my quest for the tall dark stranger. I'm a sucker for romance and a good story; and I'm getting there. Because the wheel of life is turning and fire horses are riding it, fiercely, turning the clouds and mixing the spirits, getting the moon and the sun a little bit closer to each other. Solitude is an illusion to dive in for a while, while the wheel of fortune turns.

In the meantime, I float on these winds of change, giving into the movement. I optimistically and unconditionally surrender on life, while listening to the sound of the chariot vanishing under a cloud.

The Hermit

13. THE HERMIT: CALYPSO AND HER SET OF SKINS

The Hermit went into his solitude carrying only a bright lamp. He is bringing light into the darkness. All great saints go into solitude to meet God, spirits, ghosts, or themselves. There is no greater teacher than loneliness.

If you search on Google who was the Goddess of Solitude, the result is Calypso. Solitude, the only friend that never gives up on you. Whoever has a mobile phone can just dive in the media, search for interaction and distraction, search for a long-gone Ulises. A lost desire or just a faithful chat companion. Solitude is a matter of loss.

Still, she is there every time you turn your back. Behind the smoky screen of the phone we are utterly and tragically alone. Our beautiful nymph wants us all for herself. When the curtain falls at the last act of our daily rituals, all the actors are gone home. Stripped to the bone, cold and shivering I hug my invisible friend. I really love my solitude, and unlike most of the people I grew fond of her.

It took me a while to accept this uninvited guest. At the beginning, she was just lurking in the room waiting for somebody else to come, a door to open and to make hear disappear in the darkness of the soul. Running away from loneliness is a form of art and for some of us it is a form of survival. Killing time between two spaces, humans, or encounters.

The first time I stumbled into her I was living at a boarding school. I was 14, and we were all sleeping together, eight girls in a room with one meter distance between the beds. You can be so alone around people… Especially when you don't know them, and you don't care about talking or sharing experiences. I remember just staring at the corners of the ceiling, shrinking, and coming towards me like a sharp weapon, choking me.

We had to share the bathroom, so we all showered in the same place, and there were no curtains. The shared femininity left no place for intimacy - white naked bodies with newly grown puberty hair, foaming bubbles of shampoo and closed eyes, turned backs, flesh and water. Solitude comes in many forms, even in the deepest forms of closeness. Hidden in the soap bubbles, she just pops.

Every time I moved in a new place this anguishing anxiety hit me. I was hyperventilating and not being able to sleep. Walls closing on me, the suffocation, the loss of landmarks.

I moved to Greece just before the tourist season started in March. It was the rainy, cold season. I was living on a top of a crest, in an abandoned hotel. It was just me, the dogs and the cats. And a deep raven at the bottom of it where I found the rough tumultuous sea. In the morning, the help boy came to give me a hand in opening the troglodyte houses doors, bringing the sun and the air inside and talking out the moulded mattresses. Solitude has a smell, the one of closed air in non-ventilated rooms. She also smells like burning ideas, insomnia, and shivering fear.

In that moist and rainy island it was also cold. I assumed that if I came to Greece the weather would be always beautiful, so I didn't bring any warm clothes - big mistake! Being alone and cold is the most terrifying thing. My room was a tiny piece situated above the reception of the hotel and it had a proportionally small window. I spent my evenings hiding in there, just because the hills had the ghosts of my fear, just looking at the restless sea down the hill and the illusionary boats like Miyazaki's Spirited Away ships. Boats carrying phantoms of light out there on the sea. Calypso waiting for Ulises's boat to dock on the shore.

When I could finally sleep, the mornings were rough, because when you wake up in an unknown place you must find your ground and your lost habits. Soledad – this snake, a beautiful green Amazonian one that is changing his old skin to a new one. The whole experience begins when you leave the scales of an old you, the beloved scale of your experience and attachment, and you go out naked in a new set of skin.

While knitting this new set of glorious scales, you may feel cold and strange to yourself. Lost and Lonely. That moment when the process is done, when you take out your own skin to put it back in a new way, more comfortable and cosier to keep you warm. Adaptation to a new situation in your life takes away the solitude, for a while!

Every time you feel lost and lonely and desperate, just remember that you own soft tissue of epithelial cells is hugging you right now and holding you tight.

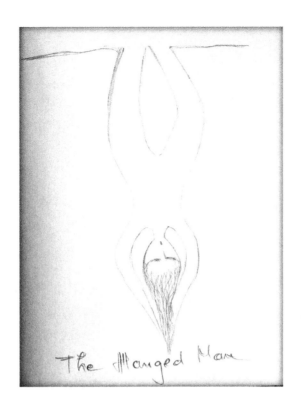

The Hanged Man

14. THE HANGED MAN: THE MAGIC OF AN OPEN DOOR

The Hanged Man is upside down - inviting you to change perspective on things that you might be stuck in or a suspended action, an awaiting. It's an invitation to let go. Cut the cord!

When I was a kid, I was waiting for Mum to come from work, and the sign was the banging sound of the door while opened. When she arrived home, she always had something for us in her bag. It was the moment when the whole house started to vibrate in the loud music of our voices. Imagine baby birds in a nest staying there with mouths wide open, waiting for mum to bring them a nice slice of a juicy insect. Waiting for that bird of prey.

We were not raised in solitude, but in a joyful gathering of a tribe who lived in small rooms during cold winters. They say your first 7 years of childhood are defining for your later self. So, if the inner child becomes your destiny, I will be the first one to fail the life proof of loneliness.

Later, when I went to college, I was hanging around with my friend Oana. When she was off for the weekend, I was really bored to death in the dorm. The weekend was dull and grey and all I was expecting was for her to bust on that door. I remember a day when it was my turn to go home and I came back with a night train by 6 o'clock in the morning. She was waiting for me, wearing blue laced panties that she just bought, high heels and a silk T-shirt. She put music on and opened a bottle of Martini. An open door is so exciting, no matter on which side you are placed…

Many years later, I moved to Paris. I had no logical explanation for my decision. I just felt like it. The apartment was behind a patio, on the fourth floor, with no elevator. It was guarded by a huge wooden door that closed automatically, that squeaked when open and its slam sounded like Thor banging his hammer. In the beginning, I had no job and I used to spend my time reading books, watching TV, and waiting for my partner to come home. He was working in a restaurant and the night shifts lasted until midnight. Sometimes, he was staying around later with the colleagues drinking or sniffing cocaine. I never understood why people in the restaurant industry feel that urge of partying like rock stars. Inside this type of business, there is the eternal dialectic of the master and the slave: I serve you, therefore I become you. A whole industry of pleasing others based on the equality postulate and fed by tons of white silky powder.

The everyday ritual: the door slams. 1 o'clock in the morning and my hearts jumps happily, like a puppy waiting for the master to come home. I hear his footsteps on the wooden stairs. We kiss, exchange a few words. He is hungry. He cooks eggs with cheese, we watch TV for half an hour, and we go to bed. We cuddle and I finally go to sleep. When we moved out of the apartment, my only nostalgic feeling was dedicated to that sound of the slamming door, like the theatre bell announcing that the actors are ready to play and the audience is silently waiting for the plot.

Waiting is such a big part of our lives, it's the gap between now and then. We wait silently for someone to come and save us from our solitude. We wait for something: a door to open and all oceans to flow into the room until they crush your body on the floor and you cannot breathe. We can be waiting for that stranger to come and swipe us off our feet, make us feel unique and amazing, the best persons on his planet. We wait for a miracle to happen.

But what if the wrong person opens the door and all our expectations crush on the knob? We keep on waiting because hope dies last…

What if you went out there into the world and started opening the doors you chose to open? *"Go out in the woods, go out. If you don't go out in the woods nothing will ever happen and your life will never begin."*, says Clarissa Pinkola Estés. A part of growing up is choosing our own battles - the door knob that fits your envies, the wood that carves your soul in a specific way, and the garden behind the gate that nourished your lips with sweet nectar. There is no shame in pleasure, there is no guilt in choosing the opportunities that suit us or in opening the doors within our envies and desires. Stop waiting, go into the woods, open the door to this enchanted forest of yours!

The last door to open is an invisible one. It makes no

noise, it is a door into the understanding of the Self. You need no forcing, no robbing for this one, just time and patience. Magically, at some point it opens itself, because all the pathways of our search and expectations take us there.

"What you seek is seeking you!" (Rumi)

15. THE MOON: UNDERWATER LOVE

The Moon is a symbol of intuition, dreams, and the unconscious. It invites you to connect with your femininity, to the water movements and to the goddess within.

When I first stepped into a Yoga studio, I took a class of Power Yoga with a hyperactive teacher and a mix of loud music and sweaty bodies. It was something between Yoga and Pilates, cardio training, and heart attack. I nearly died!

61

But, at the end of it, we did some   relaxation exercises while listening to some Tibetan gong music. In moments like these, you feel squashed, but free and proud that you survived. All that cardio was liberating, and I liked it.

Every week, I had to cross Paris for my hour of Power Yoga. You do the poses, you sweat, and you nearly die. Think about those sports junkies who hit the gym three times a day. I can definitely understand their cause. I am doing my warrior yoga workout surrounded by crop tops, leggings, and sweaty gorgeous bodies. As a kid, I hated my body. I had no interest in it and, especially, no praise for it. All that mattered were the books, the ideas, and the dreams. My body was there just to remind me that I was human.

At the end of the class, we usually do a standing shoulder pose and my belly rolls down towards my chin. In that moment, I usually close my eyes. I still hate my body, but now for a different reason, for not fitting in. I kept on going to that class, packed with wannabe Instagram stars and ex-models, middle-aged ballerinas and posh housewives. I was escorting my body on a walk of shame. I was secretly enjoying the adrenalin rush of cardio, the relief of the senses at the end of the class. At that time, there was nothing that made my heart jump out of my chest, so that was definitely the only one hour a week where I felt completely alive, such as close to dying or after sex.

My teenage version would have never hanged out with this kind of crowd. She would have for sure treated them as a gang of chickens, brain washed and booty obsessed, female objects or frustrated wives. My younger self would have displayed no pity for them. She would have hated them from the start, cruelly judging them as the opposite of all her empowered female ideal! Beauty is no feminist but it has power. This is my later self's conclusion on life. A beautiful woman is as much as we can get closer to God.

Many yoga teachers say *"make space in your body"* and you are on your mat thinking *"hey, I want to make this space disappear - the heaviness of my hips, my twisted intestines, my love handles"*... Why should I make space for all of that? For sure, my goal is not an expanded Buddha body of abundance. I want this space to disappear! A woman is not supposed to be taking any space! It is quite immoral and not aesthetic! We are taught by society that we must be quiet, cute, and caring. We are meant to make space for others, to create nests for kids or lovers. We are supposed to stay slim, small and delicate in order to fit as a genie in a man's pocket.

Maybe that was the point: if we are not allowed to expand in the outer world, the inner world comes as an exit option. I wonder what happens with this socially crushed bodies, what happens to the liver and the spleen...? What if you push too much, and the spleen spills inside, like a river of sorrow? What if your heart shrinks as a sundried tomato and she can hold love only on the edges of her wrinkles? I believe the heart can hold memories just like the brain. Memory without the Heart is like Brain without Nostalgia.

Expanding your universe from the inside - what a beautiful promise! I can already see an enormous aquarium, full of mermaids, otters and penguins living inside. So much room for small islands, where you can stop and rest staring at the sun, watch baby crabs crawling in the sand. When you do that, there are no rules, because you can make place for anything you like if it suits your heart. I love water, so for me it would look like an underwater   paradise, where you can slide between algae and seahorses and still be able to have coffee with a friend in an underwater cafeteria. There will be great humpback whales jumping around, vocalizing songs for which I will be the echo. When you tell a woman she is a whale, normally it does not sound like a good thing. But if I visualize the whales, I see magnificence and grace and only the ocean can mirror that.

In yoga, the anatomic location of the soul is in a small space beneath your heart. If I look inside myself, I see a garden with cherry trees, people, animals and birds running around free.

16. THE SUN: STARING AT THE SUN

The Sun is life itself, its energy and vitality. It reflects a time of physical energy and optimism. The Sun is the definition of Youth. It is the life force that makes the world go round!

One summer, I was in Mallorca for the holiday. I used to lay all the time on the beach under an umbrella that often flew away with the wind. My neighbours were a couple of old Germans who spent their days in oiling their brown sparkling skin and drinking beer while I was swimming.

I was reading Esther Perel's books about sexuality in a couple, but with no hope that maybe I can change something in my love life. I used some monoi oil for my burned face that smelled like cake. I always burn my face on the first days by the sea. So, when I was going out for a swim, I put on my straw hat and my big black sunglasses and I just floated. Near the beach there was a bridge and, at the bottom of it, there was a round shaped restaurant. During lunchtime is was packed with tourists and loud kids. One afternoon, I decided to have lunch there at 2 PM, after the rush hour. I took my yellow linen shirt, my tote bag and, of course, my straw hat soaked in sea water. The waiter welcomed me like he had never seen a single girl having lunch by herself! I felt shy, so I took a seat at a table for two in a corner. The waiter followed me and suggested to change the seat. He said: *"from here, you can look at the sea"*. In that moment, I saw myself in the skin of a mysterious stranger, burnt by the sun and with her skin sparking the monoi scent. During summertime, my green eyes are like sea water. In that second, the green-eyed woman became the illicit subject of desire. Another waiter came and said that someone is offering me an ice cream. The whole scene was so unreal! They all wanted to please that person I didn't recognize, to dazzle her, just because her loneliness was longing for something so appealing that they could not resist.

I have always found heat so erotic to that point that is becomes indecent. It is like all tears of sweat are the mark of a shouting orgasm of the skin, melting and decomposing under the sun. Summer is the most decadent season of all, and I understand now what my two German neighbours were doing on the beach, shimmering into the sweet light. They were masturbating! Sun means youth and the beach is a massive orgy of oily bodies, scared by time or blessed by it, a mix of illusions that wear sunscreen, a predator mood in slow motion laying in the sand. Wearing sunscreen!

Two of Cups

17. TWO OF CUPS: THE PISCES THAT SWAM IN A VOLCANO

Two of Cups means melting through the force of water, exchanging cosmic energies. This card announces romance – that moment when two become one.

When I was living in downtown Bucharest in a small studio, I worked as an Event Planner always tired of losing the weekends. This industry revolved around weddings and baptizes. It felt like working in a circus with fireworks, musicians, doves, balloons and dancers. Sometimes, by 2 AM during Saturdays, we had to go to the event place and gather the leftovers of the decorations, the satin bands on the chairs and recover the rest of the money the client owed us. I was similar to a little mobster searching for his tax.

I felt tired of this and mostly, I felt unhappy. One day I took a piece of paper and wrote a list of things that would make me joyful. First two words were Sun and Sea. So, I decided to listen to my pen and I moved out to Santorini Island in Greece, found a job as a Hotel Manager in Oia.

When we arrived there, we were a couple of Romanian girls to work for the same employer. Undeclared work, of course, and when they had people from the tax department checking the hotels, we had a man spying on them from the top of the hills and calling us to hide away. We were playing Cowboys and Indians, and because I love games, I thought it was so much fun!

I remember that when we arrived in Oia, there was nobody – only dogs and empty streets. It looked like an abandoned island. We walked on small paved wet streets, closed windows, deserted white houses with blue sheds and I was wondering what kind of mess I got myself in this time. Suddenly, in the middle of a square, near an orthodox church, we stumbled upon a concrete wall, and behind it, there was a huge void falling into a sea of deep dark blue water. The Aegean Sea was there waiting for me, and my heart jumped straight into it. The moment when you have this impression of belonging to something unknown though familiar. Everything made sense! I was there to wait for this island to bloom and there was no other place in the world that I was supposed to be in.

My hotel was a in a small village of cave houses, all at the end of Oia, a very famous travellers' spot, at the sunset point where all tourists come to take Instagram-able pictures and clap at the sunset. It gave an outstanding panoramic view of an extremely erotic moment where the sun spreads his light at dawn on the Aegean Sea.

The whole island architecture is white and curvy, like straight out of a pottery class. All the roundness of Mother Earth was put into this troglodyte caves. When I moved there, I didn't realize that I was the only tenant of the hill, so I was afraid of the winds, the rain and the loneliness. It was cold and humid, and I brought only summer clothes, because in my mind, Greece was sunny all year long (totally a myth!). Some of the cave houses were flooded by the storms, moist winter and me and another employee we supposed to take everything out. The mattresses smelled bad in their closed space, like mould due to water stagnation. When you let nature take over, in wintertime everything goes back to the earth and his roots, decomposing human life remains upon which germs and worms create life again.

Meanwhile, I was living alone on a cliff and, in front of me, there lied the Aegean Sea with a volcano sleeping by. The island was half-moon shaped because the other half went under the sea after the volcano erupted ages ago. It left place for darkest shade of blue I have ever seen. While going swimming I had a few meters of clear water. There I had my eyes on the rocks, sea urchins and small fish. Besides that, there was the blue void hosting the other part of trunked island.

I used to swim towards the black abyss, look at the ultramarine void, listening to my heartbeats of fear in front of this immense unknown water. I know that all my fears are ultramarine blue coloured. I never imagined that living near a volcano is such a powerful experience; I felt connected to this energy and all my emotions went savage. I hit bipolar states at least twice a day, enraged higher than ever, relaxed more than ever and loved like never. Because of the fire.

I blame it on the volcano, though this man turned my head around unexpectedly. He was an intern student and we worked together. He was a blonde Greek God, walking carefree with the ease of youth. *"Tall and tanned and young and lovely"*, the male version of the girl from Ipanema. I always loved to choose my men, as they were the object of my curiosity and admiration. He intrigued me with that wondering mind and spirit that I always appreciated. He challenged me in a feline playful way. I received my present from that volcano: a drop of flame. I was on the most beautiful island on the world and a love story popped.

Since childhood, we have this longing for romance. At first, there is a charming prince. Then, it gets more complex and confused when you encounter a real man. Like your human incomplete self will find at some point his soulmate. And you spent your time blaming your chipped soul on the absence of another. But he was there.

We started dated and drinking together, nights were composed of endless talks, recreating the world, listening to music, teasing each other, debating and arguing in the morning when we were too drunk to handle our emotions… We were like two demons, tearing each other apart, sharing convictions and passions. The volcano was nearby. We were both born in March, Neptunian lunar characters. He spoke my language and I spoke his, we were searching inside another pieces of common words. Together we drank the whole hotel bar and we spent nights of endless stories. He was seeing in me things I did not dare to see. Two Pisces jumping from the water into the night starry sky.

When the full moon was out, we used to wander around Santorini's houses, on their roofs like cats jumping from a rooftop on another. The moon was liquidly dropping into the sea, caressing the white walls, like cold white ghosts dancing in the magic of the night. The air was cold and moist, our skin was pale under the moonlight.

I used to love a beach called Katharos. Catharsis is Greek means purification and I heard that on that beach there were left to die hundreds of leprosy sick people ages ago. It was a hidden wild beach, with rocks, volcanic sand and not many tourists. All they had on this wild beach was some swimming rubber rings for the fun of passengers or mermaids. One day, we were together on the beach and he went swimming out in the high waves. He was jumping in rubber ring, half human, half fish. I just watched from the shore as he was gliding in the waves: the ease and the joy, this floating moment of pure youth and recklessness. He was just being.

I always hoped that this is the best memory of him, and I'm the one who's keeping it. Like you hold somebody's deepest secret with you forever. I hoped that, one day, when he would be tired of life's challenges, he would come towards me and reclaim his secret that I kept safe for so long.

The High Priestess

18. THE HIGH PRIESTESS: THE GOVERNMENT OF GRANDMAS

Ten years after my adventure in Santorini, I travelled to Athens to visit my queer photographer friend, but also my first experience azt a yoga retreat in a lost village somewhere in Greece.

My Agape, Erikkos, had a boyfriend younger than him, highly attractive and fun. We felt like happy tree friends, laughing. The words became syllables and songs. Like birds in the morning, it was not about the content, but more about the musical line. Sharing happiness in onomatopoeia is such a monkey business. We were laughing about the similarity of our grandmothers. My Grandma Flower always walks with me in life and makes me have the best encounters. Greek and Romanian grandmothers wear a scarf on the head, black clothes and know everybody. For example, if you encounter a grandmother in a village, she will definitely ask you *"to whom do you belong to?"* even if she already knows the answer. My life's conclusion I think it will be that the world should be ruled by Grandmothers. And we would definitely live in a better place. A Government of Grandmas wearing black. Bringing pies to work. Knowing everybody. A world that will emanate a profound perfume of childhood treats.

My friends and I had space cake (I they call it like that because it's made of stardust). They started playing with each other, tickling each other like kids. I was watching them with a certain nostalgia – I was missing this proximity with somebody, this lightness of being... Errikos, whom I haven't seen see for 2 years, told me that he felt like in a time machine. Like it was yesterday! I answered with a banality and I said time is subjective. The only valid time wrap is being knitted by dedicated grandmothers and it goes straight to childhood to a place where you truly belong to somebody. The following morning, I left in a hurry because my taxi came to take me to the yoga retreat. I was so excited – maybe there were the remains of our special dessert the day before! I was euphoric! My driver and I were both wearing protection masks and the air conditioner made the air unbreathable. We left Athens and in front of us the red dirty hills and olive trees were expanding their kingdom at our feet.

In Greece, I always felt like home. An organic state that I belong to this red

dirt, as my bones are almost pink from the sand from which I rose. The retreat was beautiful, between the mountain and the silver sparkling Aegean Sea. I don't know why   happiness   is   hard   to   be   put   in   words.

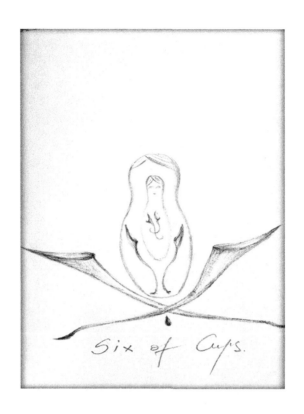

19. SIX OF CUPS: DANCING WITH STRANGERS

The Six of Cups is the nostalgia of a lost time. Proust's Madeleine. This card takes you back to the happy memories from your past.

"My kind of town, Chicago is

My kind of town, Chicago is

My kind of people, too

People who smile at you"

(Frank Sinatra)

Jazz on the streets, blues, amazing blue water and windy snows. I knew nothing about the Chicago before moving there. It was just after college when a friend of mine asked me if I wanted to move there for an internship in Hotel management. *"Hell, why not?"*

I remember passing through Chicago, as it was also my first time going to the United States. I was taking the Greyhound to go to Minneapolis. We stayed in a park and watched baby rabbits playing in the grass with so much amazement. Then we spent the night in the Greyhound station with shady people and diet Pepsi cans. Everything was so new and smelled so bad. I promised myself to go back. And I did it with a couple of friends from college. They knew some boys living there and they let us sleep over by the time we found an apartment. During my first day there, they played a prank on us and pretended breaking in the house, kicking the door shouting: *"Open the fucking door!"* I froze to death, hanged on to a knife and prayed for our souls. I felt like the trapped mouse, helpless. Then, the boys started laughing, telling us it was a joke. Too late for that, the fear was already there. I realized how fragile we are - three girls, miles away from home, complete strangers in the windy city.

Fortunately, there was a little Romanian community that helped us in finding an apartment on Catalpa Street, not far from Lake Michigan shore. We actually rented two apartments, one for the girls and another one for the boys who came along two days after our arrival. I remember first night we had no furniture, just some cardboard and some inflatable mats. We smoked cigarettes and had some wine, dozed off and waited to see what the cat brings in. Tomorrow.

I worked as an intern in the biggest hotel in Chicago. We were supposed to hostess the steakhouse restaurant and lounge. The best part of the job were the love concerts in the evening. There were two singers, Anthony and Kimberly. Anthony was all about Jack the Knife, a Sinatra impersonator with a nice black and white prohibition costume and the matching shoes. Kimberly was more close to Duke Ellington and Ella Fitzgerald's style. I was so happy that my whole heart was dancing to the music. The job was dull, but the music was amazing! The exit button that transported me to Old Chicago town in the sixties. I finished the evening shift with bluesy tunes in my head smelling like disgusting rich old folks cigars from the lounge. By 11 PM, we were all at home, gathered around cocktails, vodka, Malibu, rum, pineapple, orange and eventually wine.

Sometimes, Barb the bartender made me Starbucks take away cups, Keokee coffee with Kaluha liqueur and Bailey's, and I used to sip my "to go" on the bus, on my way home. By the time I got home, I was in the mood, for partying. The situation was exceptional: a bunch of Romanians living in Chicago, both an adventure and a vacation. Work was mandatory but unimportant. Once, after a heavy drinking night, we took out the inflatable mats, crossed the highway at 5 AM between cars, and went out to Michigan Lake for a dive. We had a friend who didn't know how to swim and we put him on a mat and we forgot him there. There are no tides on Lake Michigan, but that mat just fled away with our scared friend, waving at us to take him back. When you are young, you don't realize that danger is close and most of the time faith and luck bring you back to the shore. Our friend was lucky, as one of us was a hell of a swimmer.

When I started working in the hotel, we had a private convention, International Mister Leather for all gay and lesbian people out there, transgender, leather strings addicts.

A happy exhibition of butt cheeks and BDSM fans. The hotel was a show of leather glam in the kinkiest way. Apparently, one of the housemaids resigned after trying to clean a room with a naked guy in a cage. We had a couple of gay boys who came in the restaurant wearing only leather strings on their velvety chairs and asking for their preferred waiter, Maria. She was crazy and fun, although she warned us she could be "a bitch on wheels". They loved her rough tobacco smoker voice. Maria used to have a shot of weed from her pipe in the parking lot of the hotel every day. She was getting in the mood for customers. I admired so much the waiters in the restaurant - they were performers, artists of pleasing people, juggling with the right word for the wright glass of wine. They had a feel of people, an instant glimpse of their characters, of their secret boundaries and their hidden pleasures. I was impressed by them.

Maria was my friend. She adopted me and used to call me Maggie Girl. *"Hey, Maggie Girl, did you got drunk again last night? Baby girl, you have to stop drinking! You are getting fat!"* She took me to eat onion rings at White Castles, a mythical local fast-food chain or to eat Lithuanian food at her mother's place. Her mother had an obsession for owls and the whole house was packed of small and big, wooden or crystal glass owls. Maria was a 60 year old hippie woman, and she used to walk around naked on her porch, for the joy of her neighbours. She took me to Florida for my birthday, we rented a convertible and when I got all sunburned she laughed so hard at me. She was my American Mum and friend.

Barbara was at the bar. She walked fast paced, almost like a man, with her blonde hair, pink lipstick her very loud laugh. The laugh was a part of her character. She knew everybody, and she had her habitual customers. One of them was an extraordinarily rich real estate investor who each night brought a different escort girl with him at the bar. Barbara made sure that he always had his glass full and, by the end of the night when the escort left, it was Barb who was taking him to his room, all lame and passed out. For rich lonely people, hotel employees are like family or babysitters. Anyway, he tipped well, so everybody was happy.

Most of my friends were working in the hotel, except for two boys who were Taxi drivers in Chicago. For an immigrant, being a taxi driver is the next best thing. The boys had funny stories about Sunday morning customers passing out in the car. One of them lived a one less funny story. South Chicago was the place to avoid when you drive a taxi. It was the most dangerous area of the city, the worst slum area, the black ghetto. The passenger of his taxi asked for a ride in this area and our friend drove him, but at the end of the ride, he took out a gun, pointed out at the driver's face and told him he's getting down without paying. And he did. Just another day at the office…

In Chicago, being White or Black made a difference. I never felt like this before, we never had that at home, there was no melting pot in Romania. It felt weird and unreasonable. But it was there, like an electrical tension. People has some unsolved history issues and that was more than enough. Racism and reverse racism doing a tango.

That year, the autumn was long and golden. I learned a new expression: Indian summer. From all the seasons, that is the best one. Soft yellow leaves on the front yard of industrial red bricks homes, nice wind from the lake and a smooth heat. The city was a lizard sitting under the sunbeam, enjoying an eternal summer. Almost. I started to get used to Chicago, walking around with my headphones and listening to Jacques Brel, Edith Piaf and Tori Amos. I was enjoying the bus to Michigan Lake, speeding on the lake shore while watching the sunset, in a purple velvet glitter. Spending some time in a place is the same as spending time with people. We get the hang of it… and you start loving them.

20. THE STAR: BLAME IT ON MY GIPSY SOUL

The Star shines above you to show you your path to self-discovery. Stars point north to travellers, to the gypsies and the bohemians. You have nothing to fear!

It was June when I moved to Paris. I started my new life with vacation, a smooth intro to my French life... *"Summertime and the living is easy."*

I was embarking on a couple adventure: meeting my partner's friends, family and indulging ourselves into new habits. Soon after the summer, I had to search for a job. I had an accent as I was a Romanian immigrant and I had no valid working passes. Still, I was an immigrant of a very special status: gipsy. At that time, for most French people, there were no specific differences between Romanians and gipsies. We were the same, swimming in a sea of stereotypes and fears of others. Rroma people were pick-pocketers and singers in the metros, living on the streets and stealing all they could steal. When people asked me where do I come from because my accent was more than obvious, I simply used to say that I'm Romanian. Even though the answer was also simple, the "aah…" followed by silence was a polite version of "oh, my God…" People stayed polite, but I could feel the awkwardness.

With time, my heart started to shrink in front of the question of my origins. I was waiting for a reaction with impatience and fear. I remember that even talking on the phone was so anguishing that at some point I was losing my words, my voice and I was starting to mumble idiotically. The time for introduction was short. "Hi, I' m Romanian". Similar to a gipsy goddess with coloured skirt that took her baby out for a begging session in front of the Louvre. Who later your wallet on line 13 and who could be also found in Porte de Clignancourt proposing her sexual dexterity and ability. Her skills are various, so I wonder which one do you prefer? I will bet for the sexual ones. I remember I met a friend from collage on a terrace in Montmartre and we were having coffee, so I was talking about being Romanian and he interrupted me and said "Shhh! Don't say out loud that we are Romanian!" The trauma was too big for him. In social psychology, this reaction is called cognitive dissonance and it means holding contradictory beliefs. According to this theory, when two actions or ideas are not psychologically consistent with each other, people do all in their power to change them until they become consistent. I was hustling to adapt to my inner gypsy.

It was not a melting pot as it was in the United States, it felt different. I felt strange, I felt lost, and disappearing under the grey block of gipsy stereotypes I was trying to break around me. I had to explain, prove, and create myself. I was mild, educated and polite, proving my worth in the reign of humans: Europeans / French.

Finding a job became a hustle. Nobody wanted me, my accent, my origins, and my assumed immorality. I spent my time walking on the streets of Montmartre, watching people and places. The city became my friend, keeping me safe from insanity and loneliness. I was a lonely traveller on the paved streets of Montmartre, bathing in his beauty and dynamic, a mixture of made-in-China souvenirs, fake artists, consumer tourists, students, beggars and gypsies. Walking kept me sane: out of the apartment, out of my head, out of my doubts and fears. I was facing the impossible and moving was my only way to fled disaster. I watched yoga videos, I was doing mediation and reading self-help books. Most probably, self-help books never helped me, because when you go through suffering, you just walk it out. Ignoring the pain is like ignoring a white amazing elephant in your backyard. Pain is there for a reason. And *"the wound is the place where the light gets in"*, as Rumi beautifully said it.

With time passing, Paris become my best friend. The paved streets, the coffee places, Jardin de Luxembourg and Montmartre, la Seine. The perfect companion for solitude. Paris never let me down, because the romance is so big and this lover is a unique, multifaceted, and fascinating charmer.

21. THE QUEEN OF WANDS: EMBRACING THE COLOURS IN YOUR LIFE

The Queen of Wands encourages you to be fearful. To take action, embody your dreams, be courageous and pursue your vision.

In French, Château Rouge means Red Castle. It's also a metro stop in Paris and a neighbourhood. When I had to move there, I checked on Google maps and saw that it was close to Montmartre. I was thrilled! When I arrived there for the first time, it was December. It was snowing, and the streets were full of a mixture of silky snow and sticky dirt. I carried my bag on the paved street during midnight. I didn't imagine Montmartre this way, but it seems that at night all cats were grey. During daytime, I noticed that all cats were...black. Château Rouge was the African district of Paris. Surprisingly, it is just few minutes away from touristy Montmartre, but was nothing like it. We were living in Little Africa in Paris: in Togo, Mali, Nigeria , Senegal or Cameroun.

We were living in one of the poorest neighbourhoods of Paris, and that gave all its glam. The neighbourhood was glamorous because of the wax shops, the colourful dressed mamas that sometimes carried theirs bags on their heads. Most Paris is dressed in black and blue, sad grey colours straight out of the urban spleen. In here, people are sparkling exotic suns on their clothes. If you want to see people wearing bright colours - yellow, pink, electric green, flowers print or mystical prints - this was the place. Also, the place to buy a purple wig, a voodoo doll, plastic shaped Virgin Marries, creams that made your skin white, lube, condoms, fake nails, exotic music CDs, old tapes and some love infusion. I often received flyers of famous marabout who pretended to cure diseases and broken hearts, tying the man to the woman or vice versa with love honey. I never tried it and I regret it now, what if it works?

Out on the streets they were selling smoked fish in banana leaves and Nigerian small eggplants, gumbo, sweet potatoes, hot boiled corn and roasted peanuts. On Saturdays, the neighbourhood is packed with Africans from all over Paris and suburbs, shopping for products that take them nostalgically home on their mother porch. Everybody's dressed up as for a big occasion. The others look on them as important because they are the significant Others, the ones that they want to impress. The Others are the eyes that understand the stories, the cultural codes, the language, their status and the symbols printed on the wax tissues.

Finding a place where you feel like belonging is not that easy in Paris. Most of the time a stranger becomes invisible in the crowds, this fine mixture of individuals becomes a sea of forgotten souls. In Chateau Rouge, the African community was regaining their bright colours, and even if I have never been to Africa in my life, a beautiful wax dress could take me in the middle of the red sunburned sands, dried herbs and baobab trees. I remember once I saw a woman walking barefoot on the street. The feet were so cracked and, at that moment, I understood that she spent most of her life walking with no shoes on hot ground which almost cooked her skin in serpent scales. I felt her pain of walking on concrete streets.

Sometimes, police barged in the illegal market and street vendors were running fiercely with their fake Vuitton bags and contraband sunglasses. Behind them, they used to leave their cardboard improvised stand. After a rainy day, the cardboard became soft, melted dirt and got mixed with the rest of unsold fruits and vegetables tossed away. The neighbourhood was dirty, and people would complain. They accused the policemen of playing a ridiculous „ballet" with the illegal vendors. They played a hide and seek or cat and mouse game, with no concrete purpose. Five minutes after the police raid, the vendors were back on their workspace, the street.

The street was the office of the working girls: African, Chinese or Eastern European. At night-time, the sideways were animated with these groups of girls, talking mostly in English, listening to music and dancing. I was seeing the guys asking the prices, charming them. Most of the time you could feel the embarrassment and the shame. I tried not to judge, and I never lifted my eyes, pretended not to see them. I always looked at the girls when I came home late at night.

They were my neighbours, and it was mutual. I felt so lucky that life didn't brought up this situation in my destiny. I always thought like one's destiny can be fragile, and we are never at shelter. Some of the girls were young, maybe minors and I read in the press that some of them they were related to prostitution network from Nigeria ruled by women. "The Mamas" were tempting these young girls with a better life in France, going to school, working in hairdressing saloons, waitressing, but instead they put them on the street to hustle. "The Mamas" had an association called „The Authentic Sisters" - isn't that ironic? They were actually mothers or stepmothers in real life. This is one sisterhood that I would not vote for.

Sometimes in the hallway of our building we found used condoms, because the girls had no place to go and they used the inner courtyard of the blocks as office. People were not happy. As they were not happy seeing the crack users down in the metro station. But people never thought about their chance and destiny that did not brought this option into their own chart of fate. People should be happier!

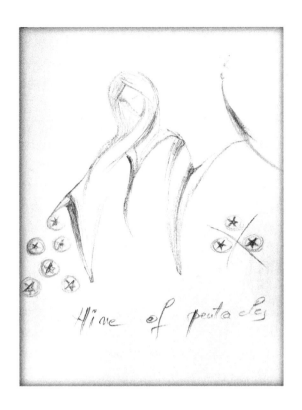

22. NINE OF PENTACLES: CINDERELLA AT THE OPERA

The Nine of Pentacles shows a well-dressed woman who is maybe going to the Opera. Glamour, opulence, abundance, and luxury - how could we resist it?

I was living in Paris for a few months now. No working papers, desperate for a solution. My friend Alina suggested going back to college. Yeah sure! I was 30 back then! But suddenly, the idea didn't sound that bad. I started my research and found two universities that looked interesting, filed my candidate papers with the money I gained…at a poker game. Alina told me they will never accept me at

Descartes University, as I didn't have the good pedigree. Still, against all odds, I got admitted at the European Sociology Master's degree. Life is like a poker game: sometimes you win only because of a good bluff.

The Master's degree was almost only for foreign students. We were some sort of lab experiment, a mini political melting plot. There was a Bulgarian, a Russian, a Swedish of Serbian parents, a Spanish, a Chinese, a few French and I... The Romanian. Going back to school was fun, as my inner geek was thriving and my outer extrovert was driving my colleagues into some nice moments, including a lot of alcohol and a little bit of memory loss.

During night time, I was working part-time as a hostess in a restaurant near the Opera. I was placing people on soft velvet couches in an Art Nouveau palace of opulence. The customers were rushing in sipping wine while sharing huge platters of seafood. I was checking also the coats in the entrance hallways, learning to read a book by its cover. The label on the coat was pretty much telling the story of a rich, a poor or an escort girl. Some of them were tourists, wearing unknown brands of clothes, some of them there were wearing Zara, which for me meant they were the working people with a good pay check who want to enjoy the Parisian lifestyle, but not rich enough to afford the house in the suburbs. Then, there were the dead animal fur coats that carried, besides their opulence, the smell of closed cupboards of ancient aristocracy from an old revolutionary time.

You could also see Russians with escort girls, two or three per guy, plus even more bottles of champagne on the table. In the French culture, there is a shyness towards displaying any sign of fortune and wealth. In the Eastern part of the continent, in Russia, success rhymes with all the best life can offer. Sparkles, bubbles, amazing young pink delicious bodies on velvet couches, the roman buffet of delicatessen, and a well-dressed waiter who speaks Russian and the language of flattery.

My secret wish is to be reborn in a young Russian Aeron of a wealthy family, biting with all his teeth on life's decadent pleasures. Maybe for you reading this right know, it may sound like a barbarous stereotype. Let me just keep this one experience as a personal résumé. I have always dreamed that, one night, it will be me wearing a fantastic gown, getting out if the Opera Garnier, coming out for supper. Years after, just after Christmas, I bought a ticket and went there by myself, saw half of the ballet (I'm a fan of modern ballet and opera is out of my reach and understanding) because the seat was cheap and the visibility was bad. I bought myself champagne in between the acts, enjoyed the golden walls and the crystal chandeliers of the cocktail room, the spectacular view of Paris from the balcony and the Chagal paintings on the ceiling. At the end of it, I took the metro and went back home. If I would have gone out for supper, my old colleagues would recognize me, and I would have turned back in Cinderella with a pumpkin and an unbranded coat on her back. So I spared myself from the disenchantment.

My two years in college were a funny way of becoming a Sociologist: reading and writing about extreme right parties, racism and political hate. Why do people fear other people? I wanted so bad to revenge or understand the awkwardness of being a Romanian in France. I never felt that way in Chicago. The reluctant people, the silence after the *"ohh, you're Romanian"*. I studied for two years the political speech, I listened to thousands of hours of right wing leaders' debates, and wrote my thesis on language and its role in creating reality, on fears, stereotypes and foreigners. If you think about it, language is the first thing that alienates us from ourselves. Imagine for one second what this does to others. At some point, I realized that if I pursued this field of research, my quest for an explanation on my discrimination experience will, at some point, become my destiny.

I did not care anymore and I think that's what set me free. It also set the others a little bit loose and more empathetic. When you stop being alert to all signs of prejudice, you just resonate to people on another level. Besides all our different stories, there is an indefinite state where we meet and relate.

23. EIGHT OF SWORDS: ON MONSTERS AND CHILDREN

This card symbolizes the fact that the mind can play trick on us and get us caged into our own fears and anxieties. We can end up living like a prisoner inside ourselves.

Happiness is a leap of faith. It takes a lot of courage. We are raised to stand harsh times, to listen, to obey, not to get out there and grab the biggest part of the cake and just savour it. Maybe it's a childhood's story, one when not all things that make you happy are allowed. But being happy is an act of bravery.

I wonder why after all the Zen and psychology books, the yoga, the meditation and the psychoanalysis, I still feel the pain as a constant companion for my loneliness. Am I not brave enough to face myself? My demons, and my ghosts? What is it out there that is so monstrous to meet? Where does it lie and linger? Where are you, you little crawler? Yes, you, the one who plays with my life indefinitely. The joker, the hangman!

How Freudian would it be to search the origins of the sorrow in my childhood? It seems so reductive in my opinion. Alcoholism and violence, resentment and pain. Pandora's Box scattered in my parents' home on the wool carpet. How long can grief persist, long enough to let go?

An open wound takes an eternity to heal, especially when it is around the heart. Did my heart continue to beat all this year behind an open wound? The eagle of sorrow bites from now and then little pieces of flesh. I walk the line in perfect equilibrium, I learned how to perfectly balance my pain not to fall. I'm a balanced human, but nonetheless a fallen angel.

At some point in my life, I was a school counsellor in my hometown, working with children and teenagers. With the lost ones, the disturbed, the unwanted, the unfitted and the depressed, the outlaws of the school world. I was using art therapy and storytelling to reach them. Especially in childhood kingdom, logic makes no sense and has no healing effect for nobody. Plus, I strongly believe logic has no effect on adults either.

My counselling sessions of painting were with a boy who was drawing monsters that scared his family and his teachers. The sessions were taking place in a dusty old library because the school had no funds for a special therapy place. I used to give him papers and pencils and he was drawing while I was asking random things about his life. The monsters were black, with sharp teeth and small eyes. He was calm and, while drawing, the words untangled the story. I will not tell you his secret, but just let you know that the monsters were the faces of his fears, biting sharply in this child's imaginary world.

If we were all to draw one day our fears, our shadows hunting us in the middle of the night? The fear of being abandoned, to be left alone, to be unloved and insecure? The fear of losing and the fear of dying? They would all gather together in such majestic painting. A painting to hang in the middle of a dining room…while on a diet.

Another child I met in this magical place of the library was one with ADHD diagnosis. He was living with his grandparents. Half of that generation were raised by grandparents, because the parents left to work abroad. It is a special honour to be raised by a grandparent, because he is twice wiser than the parent. The only disadvantage is that the child skips a generation of knowledge and experience. Grandparents are cool, sometimes to cool. Still, growing up without a father figure but a grandmother one I think can represent a great advantage for humanity.

This attention disorder the child suffered from can be very a difficult act. Imagine yourself in a candy shop while addicted to sugar - every piece of the space will be an attire to you. Hyperactive people want to explore the world in its details. When you put an ADHD child in a library it is the same thing as placing him in a maze of books, colours, shapes and textures. He spends his time taking the books out of the shelves just to rearrange them.

I had him choose his favourite story and tell me also his version of it. His choice was Alice in Wonderland. He was Alice, too big or too small to fit through the door to Wonderland. The symbolic door of fitting into this world of norms and prospects. While all the teachers were trying to have him stay attentive and calm, he was doing all backwards. But aren't we all inadequate at some precise point in our life? Didn't we all accidentally intersected with this child in our life without noticing it?

What stroke me was that beneath all his active and agitated self, nobody saw his suffering of not fitting in translated in violence and bad behaviour. While he was telling his versions of Alice in Wonderland, I recreated my version of the story as an answering, as a response to his riddle. In this version, the doors were at the good height for my lively friend to get inside this amazing world. That is why I love so much a good story! Stories speak directly to the heart. The more we involve the logic, the more we lose the meaning of the story. Only then Alice realizes the characters are only a pack of cards and awakens from her dream.

The key that fits your soul is a perfect story. The stories you tell yourself, the narrative of your journey, the characters you meet in your path. The Mad hatter, the lion, the tin man, the leprechauns and the dwarfs, the panther, the cat, the horse, the fairies and the fireflies.

24. THE FOOL: RANDOMNESS WITH A TWIST OF EXTRAVAGANZA

The Fool left all his human belongings, and he is walking freely and joyfully into the unexpected!

While walking in the forest, the air changes from now and then and hot waves of air come and gently touch the skin. The same sensation as when you are swimming in the sea and you feel cold currents coming and going beneath you.

It takes a second to make everything change upside down, to transform your life and who are. Buddhists call this impermanence. But how much did I change? Where did I leave that chubby shy child from my grandparents' cherry garden? Where are all these old cells disappearing, my beautiful green snake scales scattered on the soil? While trying to feel like a whole and coherent individual, where did all these avatars of me go?

Maybe right now, when I am writing, one of them is dying. Like a fallen broken angel, with no feathers, naked and tired of all the existence's expectation, and also tired of being good.

Do we cling on the memories of our past just to carefully pack the emptiness of our invisible souls? Or inexistent ones. In some nice shiny present box…

A human is like a puppet made of colourful patches, a temporary manifestation of movement's inertia, life's energy and willingness to exist. Randomness with a twist of extravaganza. Shall I accept that everything around me is happening accidentally? Scattered elements on the floors as a broken glass, into a tornado of butterflies flopping their electric blue wings.

While making sense of my life's story, I return to innocence. Into my grandparents' garden, as if I never left and life has left no scars on my pink, perfect skin. This is the whole meaning of making sense: becoming whole again. I'm not entirely broken, because I'm surrounded by the spirit of the generations of warrior ghosts of my lineage. Ancestors and animal spirits. Great goddess of everyday life. Mothers and witches.

But what if I could go back and change the whole destiny of things?

My Dad would have not become an alcoholic, would not have lost his job and become violent to Mum. I would love him to age with dignity and be a male role model for as long as he lives. I would have made Mum happy and back pain-free. I would erase the memory of violence from her and my sister's life.

I would create Margot a place where she could feel free to smoke as much cigarettes as she would.

I would have given Tin Man a heart so he could not fear to love me as I feared to love him .

I would have helped Mr. X's parents to stay together and not abandon him in the middle of his childhood, so he would never feel like being left behind ever again. He would start loving himself a little bit more.

I would had given my horse a decent funeral, instead of letting her die in a slaughterhouse after a car accident. We would be still riding fluffy nimbus on the tip of our toes.

I would have taken Grandma to the ocean, so she could have freely swam with her mermaid tail. She would have never lost her teenage son. He would have been my favourite uncle, teaching me how to play with death and get away.

What about me? What was the train I should have taken, or the door should have opened? Which key did I lost on the way?

Between people and places, I sit in a vintage black and white family picture. Not smiling, as it would look awkward. I would give myself a million soft warm hugs, because loneliness sometimes feels cold and uncomfortable. The hugs of a Mother - skin on skin. Being an adult is not an easy task and I am not that good at delivering it.

For now, I will join the Fool in his Journey, as he nothing to hold on to. He walks freely on his path because in life we can start as many times as needed. Especially in Taro!

Printed in Great Britain
by Amazon